God Can Help You *Heal*

Gregory L. Jantz, Ph.D.
with Ann McMurray

Publications International, Ltd.

Gregory L. Jantz holds a Ph.D. in counseling psychology and health services. He is the founder and executive director of The Center for Counseling & Health Resources, Inc. A frequent lecturer and guest on radio and television, Dr. Jantz is the author of more than 20 books on a variety of recovery and health topics. Information about Dr. Jantz can be found on his Web site at *www.aplaceofhope.com* or by calling toll-free 888-771-5166. He is a member of The American Association of Christian Counselors, the International Association of Eating Disorder Professionals, and the American Counseling Association.

The Center for Counseling & Health Resources, Inc. has four branches in the Puget Sound area of Seattle, Washington. The Center is known for its intensive recovery programs for those suffering from depression, anxiety, trauma, eating disorders, and addictions. A state-licensed mental health and chemical dependency agency, The Center provides services to people of all ages, covering a wide variety of mental health issues and chemical dependency treatments.

Ann McMurray has collaborated with Dr. Jantz on several projects as co-writer and is operations assistant at The Center for Counseling & Health Resources, Inc.

Scripture quotations marked NIV are taken from *The Holy Bible, New International Version.* Copyright © 1973, 1978, 1984, International Bible Society. Used by permission of Zondervan Publishing House. All rights reserved.

All other Scripture quotations are taken from the *New Revised Standard Version* of the Bible. Copyright © 1989 by the Division of Christian Education of the National Council of the Churches of Christ in the USA. All rights reserved.

Louis Weber, CEO
Publications International, Ltd.
7373 North Cicero Avenue
Lincolnwood, Illinois 60712

Permission is never granted for commercial purposes.

Manufactured in U.S.A.

8 7 6 5 4 3 2 1

ISBN-13: 978-1-4127-1379-5
ISBN-10: 1-4127-1379-X

Contents

Let Go and Let God

Let go and let God. Although they are but five simple words, they contain the essence of God's path to healing. For God is the ultimate author of healing, and letting go is a journey, especially when the pain is deep-rooted or long-term or both. It would be nice to think that our topic resonates with only a few, but the truth is that pain, sorrow, and suffering are universal realities in this world. The good news is that while the world's evils may be the source of suffering, God is the source of all healing. As you read, I ask you to believe in the power of God to overcome your problems. This book will address pain, sorrow, and suffering, but it is really about victory—the victory of God to help you find your way to healing.

Because we are detailing a wide variety of trials and struggles, not every example will match your own. You may discover, however, that through reading the chapters and examples given, you will find healing for more than you considered when you began to read. We rarely experience injury from a single source, and pain comes from many different directions. Allow God to speak to you in unanticipated ways as you move from page to page.

As much as possible, seek to place yourself within the stories you read. Look at your life, and ask God to reveal his truth to you. Wrestle with the Scriptures presented. Be alert to what God wants to show you about yourself and your suffering. You've been living with the pain for long enough, and I encourage you to use this book to move beyond it.

It is no accident that we began with an understanding of truth—who God is and who we are. In the aftermath of trauma and suffering, truth can be easy to forget. And it's no accident that this book ends with a discussion of vision—the ability to look forward into the future. A journey toward healing starts with an understanding of where we are right now. Healing is realized when we find a renewed ability to see a positive future provided for us by a loving God.

I believe in that future. I believe in it for myself, and I believe in it for you.

Gregory L. Jantz
Edmonds, Washington

Chapter One

Truth

I Will Let Go and Let God Remind Me of Who I Am and Who He Is

Have you seen them on the side of the road? On a freeway off-ramp or a city intersection? They hold up handwritten signs: "Homeless—will work for food" or "Needy—please help." In those few seconds, before you make the turn or the light changes, it's easy to see just the sign, just the circumstances. But have you ever really stopped to look at their faces, or do you accept the sign at face value? It's easy to identify them with their "condition" and whatever regrettable circumstances brought them begging for money and food. *It's so sad what people are reduced to,* you may think to yourself. God would agree.

Cathy wore her large sign at all times. It said "unworthy." She'd been instructed to make and wear this sign growing up. In the midst of a household full of other children with a distant father and a controlling mother, Cathy was the "unworthy" child. Other children in the family were given signs such as "favored" or "accepted." For reasons she could never quite grasp, which became irrelevant to her miserable situation, her mother singled Cathy out for disdain.

Meanwhile, her siblings became accustomed to their mother treating Cathy this way, and they accepted her sign as well. Terrified they should somehow end up with Cathy's sign, they subtly reinforced her sign with their own behavior toward her. Cathy could never seem to do anything right or compensate for all the faults her mother found in her. It wasn't, however, for lack of trying. You see, Cathy accepted the sign and used it as motivation to constantly try to please others, even as an adult.

Sin was an easy concept for Cathy. She was well prepared to understand herself as unworthy before God. The more she came to know Jesus, however, the greater the trouble she had with her sign. It chafed and felt uncomfortable. "But I am unworthy of you, Lord," she would protest.

"Cathy," God kept telling her, "you think the sign says 'unworthy,' but it really reads 'worthless,' and you are far from worthless." Finally, Cathy understood the incredible value God placed upon her life and her soul. Though it still feels odd, Cathy now displays her true sign: "Valued by God."

Have you ever thought about holding up your own sign? Oh, probably not "homeless," but what about "wounded," "victimized," or "abused"? Maybe "addicted," "damaged," or "struggling"? What about "bitter," "angry," or "numb"? Your sign becomes an identification card. It defines who you are by what you've done or what has happened to you. Whether you realize it or not, you wrote the sign and held it up in front of yourself. This sign appears to be the truth. After all, there is history behind the label. But it's built upon a crushing misconception: that your identity in life is limited to your life experiences. This belief may be the world's truth, but it is not God's truth.

On the path to healing, you need to know the truth of where you're starting from. When you know your beginning point, the details of the journey make more sense. After all, starting ten miles from your destination is not the same as starting a thousand miles from it. Your travels would be quite different if you began at the top of a mountain and descended, as opposed to beginning at the base and climbing straight up. Understanding the landscape helps whether you're starting from a desert or from a forest.

The signs we wear are our starting point for healing. If those labels are false, we experience false starts. In order to heal, we must truly identify ourselves so we know from where we're starting. But how can we go down the right path if we have only our inaccurate signs to guide us? The answer lies in allowing God to provide the right signs to show you where to start.

Lord, I know what I see when I
look in the mirror, but is that who I
really am? Help me see myself
through your eyes.

Let's look at some of the signs God sees when he looks at you.

Who I Am

FALLEN—"But wait," you might say. "Why do we have to start with this one? Don't I feel bad enough as it is?" It's vital to understand that God is aware of the harm sin does in your life. The sins of others wound you, and your own sin compounds the damage. This is the truth of the human condition.

Let's go back for a minute to that desert, to hauling yourself up the side of that mountain, to that journey of a thousand miles. In the aftermath of suffering and trauma, these analogies are appropriate. It takes tremendous effort to forge ahead through challenging experiences. Have the sins of others ever battered you? Has the evil in the world damaged your life? Are you ready to start on your own path to healing, even if you have an uphill road to begin with? Your answer to this last question must be "yes," for the alternative is to stay stuck where you are, enduring the pain of open wounds.

The journey to healing begins with this truth of the human condition: "All have sinned and fall short of the glory of God" (Romans 3:23). This is the landscape we live in and travel through. Trauma and suffering occur as a natural consequence of life. We don't need to go looking for it; it finds us easily enough. And we bring it along ourselves.

In a fallen world, we trip over holes of our own design and those made by others. When multiple holes confront us, we find it difficult to recognize the difference between the two kinds of holes. We blame ourselves for the holes caused by others, and we blame others for the holes we've dug. "Our role is to recognize our limits and to transcend those limits," says Dr. Henry Townsend, "by looking outside of ourselves for life" (*How People Grow*, 31). By looking outside of ourselves—that is, to God's help and insight—we are able to discern the truth. Knowing what holes are caused by others helps us avoid the trap of false guilt. Understanding what holes we dig ourselves helps us avoid the trap of denial.

False guilt happens when we assume that the holes caused by others are in some way our own fault. This often occurs with those of us who have suffered abuse or been victimized by the evil of others. We think we deserved it; we should have been stronger; we should have been able to resist; we feel somehow at fault for what was done to us. Can you identify with this feeling? Were you told by the person who mistreated you that you were to blame? As they were beating you down, did they scream that it was *all your fault?* In a fallen world, those who perpetrate evil rarely take responsibility for it. They leave the landscape pockmarked with craters, mislabeled with the names of those they hurt.

Sometimes, we run into trouble when we fail to identify the holes we dig for ourselves. They are so deep and painful that we refuse to accept our own responsibility for them. In a fallen world, the desire to overlook a personal shortfall can land us in a deep pit. While it's important to avoid false guilt, God expects us to listen to our conscience when we fail. It does us no good, and great harm, if we deny our own holes. The apostle John put it this way: "If we say that we have no sin, we deceive ourselves, and the truth is not in us" (1 John 1:8).

Yes, the truth is that each of us is a fallen individual living among fallen people. Praise God, the truth doesn't stop there!

FORGIVEN—The gospel of Jesus Christ is called Good News for good reason. Our worldly nature makes it clear why we are called "Fallen." God's divine nature makes it possible for us to be called "Forgiven." Through the sacrifice of Christ, God changes the "Fallen" into the "Forgiven." Many of us, because of sin in our lives, are all too aware of our fallen status. Because of the damage, we assume God no longer has any interest in us, that he could never forgive us, or that he doesn't love us. Nothing could be further from the truth! Yet we can become so focused on our own frailties that God's power is obscured.

After decimating his family's finances through a gambling addiction, Barry sought help. He went into counseling and, through the recovery process, reconciled with his wife and children. He heard their forgiveness but had a hard time feeling forgiven inside. He felt tremendous shame for what he'd done. His stomach dropped every time he walked into church, for he didn't feel that God had really forgiven him either. All he could think about was the damage he had caused; this was his reality. Then, he realized the restoration God was doing in his life, and this became his new focus. Barry learned an important lesson: God is willing and able to forgive our sins; this is the central theme of Scripture.

We read about our fallen status above in 1 John 1:8, which says we all fall short of God's glory, and many of us stop right there. But listen to the very next verse: "If we confess our sins, he who is faithful and just will forgive us our sins and cleanse us from all unrighteousness" (1 John 1:9). We are fallen, yes, but we are also forgiven through Christ. When God looks at us, he sees the image of his perfect Son. It becomes his sign we wear.

God is not unkind. While he wants us to understand our sin, he offers us his divine forgiveness. Just so there's no misunderstanding, John reminds us that the blood of Jesus purifies us from all sin if we confess our sins to God.

LOVED—One of the most familiar verses of the Bible speaks of God's love for us: "For God so loved the world that he gave his only Son, so that everyone who believes in him may not perish but may have eternal life" (John 3:16). When you read this verse, it says, "God so loved the *world*," but it means *you.* God loves you so much that he gave Jesus for you. This truth can be hard for people to accept. *Surely,* they think, *there must be a catch. If God really loves me, why does he let me suffer? If God really knows all about me, how can he still love me?* These questions are reasonable. From our point of view, God's love makes no sense. The key phrase here is "from our point of view." God's love is based upon his perspective, not ours; upon his nature, not ours. What about those questions? God does not promise to remove all suffering. On the contrary, he promises us suffering in this life: "I have said this to you, so that in me you may have peace. In the world you face persecution. But take courage; I have conquered the world!" (John 16:33). He promises to see us through because he is merciful and faithful. God knows everything about us and chooses to love us because he is, by his very nature, love.

Lord, you know everything about

me, and you still love me anyway.

Thank you for your love! Help me

feel it every day.

As we travel toward healing, we need to remember that we are more than fallen, more than forgiven; we are loved. This truth keeps us traveling in the right direction. God's love acts as a beacon. David, the psalmist, said it this way: "For your love is ever before me, and I walk continually in your truth" (Psalm 26:3 NIV).

When trauma and suffering threaten to remove all signs of love in your life, God is able to restore your identity as *beloved*. Though others may have harmed you and caused you to doubt that you could ever be loved, God has already demonstrated how much you mean to him through the sacrifice of Jesus. If you've damaged your life and feel unlovable, especially by God, please realize God has always loved you, and he gave Jesus to die for you even when you were fouled by your sins (Romans 5:6).

CHILD—There are few images as poignant as a mother holding her child. The mother represents nurturing warmth, fierce love, and constant protection. The child represents vulnerability and innocence. Are you able to see yourself as a child of God? Does that imply a status to which you believe you are not entitled? For many of us, this just doesn't seem possible. Rick Warren answers the dilemma this way: "God doesn't want you to become a god; he wants you to become *godly*—taking on his values, attitudes, and character" (*Daily Inspiration for the Purpose-Driven Life*, 135). And we become godly as we learn to be children in Christ.

Perhaps the reason we doubt God's love for us is because we've seen love demonstrated so poorly and imperfectly by those around us or even within ourselves. We look to family, to friends, or in the mirror for a working definition of love, and we come up short. Our love is limited, conditional, sporadic, and begrudging. It's difficult, therefore, to accept God's unlimited, unconditional, consistent, willing love. But listen to how God says he views you: "Therefore be imitators of God, as beloved children, and live in love, as Christ loved us and gave himself up for us, a fragrant offering and sacrifice to God" (Ephesians 5:1–2). You are *dearly* loved as a child of God, and he desires a *life of love* for you.

✝   ✝   ✝

Who God Is

Truth lies not just in knowing who you are but also in knowing who God is. When it's hard to comprehend how God can call you forgiven, loved, and his child, it helps to understand who God is. Oh, we are very familiar with some of the signs God wears—Creator of the universe, righteous judge, all-powerful, and all-knowing. Many of us come from a tradition in which these attributes are stressed in a vivid, accusatory tone. It can be a challenge to see the other names God has for himself.

Cathy, like many people, saw God as harsh, unrelenting, powerful yet distant. She longed to feel loved by him and always seemed to approach him tentatively, as if expecting to be surprised or punished at any moment. She couldn't grasp why her understanding of God didn't seem to line up with what she read in Scripture. It all fell into place, however, when she explored her relationship with her earthly father, an emotionally removed disciplinarian. She'd taken the image of her earthly father, puffed it up into divine proportions, and called it "God." Healing came when she allowed God to set his own parameters and define his own name.

FATHER—Children have parents, and, as a child of God, you are no exception. God is your Father. Matthew 5:45 makes it clear that we are children of our "Father in heaven." Jesus reiterated this relationship by beginning his famous prayer, often called The Lord's Prayer, with these words: "Our father in heaven . . ." (Matthew 6:9). God has established this parent-child relationship and treats us accordingly.

Even more so than earthly parents do, God desires to give us good things. His relationship with us as our Father is not distant or uncaring. Listen to Jesus in Matthew 7:11: "If you then, who are evil, know how to give good gifts to your children, how much more will your Father in heaven give good things to those who ask him!" Because God has declared himself your Father, whenever he looks at you, he sees his child. Just as a mother cannot seem to take her eyes off her newborn, God can't take his eyes off of you. Just as a mother always remembers the infant in the adult, God holds safe the reality of your innocence and your unspoiled nature. He wants you to accept yourself and come to him as that child. Jesus said, "Truly I tell you, unless you change and become like children, you will never enter the kingdom of heaven" (Matthew 18:3). God takes his parenthood very seriously; so should we. God sets his own definition; we should follow it.

God, in the midst of my pain, hold
me close and comfort me as my
heavenly Father.

SAVIOR—Because we live in a fallen world, we are in desperate need of a Savior, and God does not disappoint. He has proven himself to be the Savior to his people across the vast stretches of time. From the physical nation of Israel to the spiritual offspring of Abraham, God is Savior. David, the psalmist, put it this way: "Lead me in your truth, and teach me, for you are the God of my salvation; for you I wait all day long" (Psalm 25:5). We doubt God can be our Savior when life bruises us. We think God was nowhere around to help. Worse, we think God has turned his back on us. Let's look at the life of David, who wrote the beautiful words of Psalm 25. He was bruised by others who tried to take his life, including his own son. David was falsely accused, run out of town, attacked, and betrayed. Yet he could still call God his Savior. David is called a "man after God's own heart," but he bruised himself through his sin with Bathsheba and the death of his infant son. Yet he could still call God his Savior. Whatever circumstances you have experienced or brought upon yourself, they do not prevent God from saving you. If you cry out to him to save you, he will.

Chapter Two

Acceptance

---

*I Will Let Go and Let God Show
and Teach Me Grace*

Knowing the truth is one thing; accepting the
truth is another. Knowledge is usually gained as
insight. A light clicks on, a piece falls into place,
two halves come together to make a whole.
In that moment, you recognize truth, and it
becomes a part of you. Accepting that truth,
however, isn't always easy. Oh, you may wear the
truth, but it chafes around the neck and binds up
at the shoulders. It feels wrong, even though you
know it is right. It can be hard to accept how
much the wrongs of the past have changed your

life. It can be hard to accept that those who should have loved you didn't. It can be hard to accept that you are no different from those who wronged you. It can be hard to accept that the way you've always wanted to think about yourself isn't true. What do you do when you find it hard to accept the truth?

On the spiritual path to healing, acceptance allows you to move beyond the blockades of bitterness and blame. These roadblocks leave you stranded on the path. And no matter how hard you push against them with all of your strength, you don't move. Because of the effort you're expending, it seems as if you're accomplishing something, but you're stuck—you're not moving forward to healing.

Jim dreaded family reunions. His wife, who practically forced him to go, handled all the details. He went, if only so the kids could see their grandparents, aunts, uncles, and cousins. There were so many reasons, however, not to go: It was expensive; it took up vacation time at work; he never spent time doing what he wanted to do but what everyone else thought was important; somebody usually wasn't speaking to somebody else at the reunion; and people expected more from him than he wanted to give. Reunions were chaotic and messy. What should take 15 minutes took an hour. It was a struggle getting three sets of parents, a set of grandparents, and eight kids to do anything! These reunions tore up his insides, and he just wanted to go back home—to peace and quiet—from the moment he arrived.

But what disturbed Jim the most was spending time with his younger brother, Steve. As long as

they were with a group of people, it was okay, but
if they ever happened to be alone in a room,
things became uncomfortable. Jim preferred to
convey an adult image of calm and reasonable-
ness and create an impression of competence
and control. Steve knew better. Growing up,
Jim had treated Steve very badly. As the older
brother, Jim found Steve irritating and bother-
some, and he resented the way Steve always
seemed to catch a break from their folks because
he was younger. Jim made up for it by being hard
on Steve himself. Looking back over the years,
Jim had come to realize he'd been a jerk. Whenever they were together, alone together, he always
had the urge to say he was sorry. He hated
reunions because he never could bring himself
to do it.

Don't Miss God's Grace

"See to it that no one fails to obtain the grace of God; that no root of bitterness springs up and causes trouble, and through it many become defiled" (Hebrews 12:15).

As was said in the first chapter, most of the pain in our lives comes as a consequence of the sins of others wounding us and our own sin compounding the pain. To heal, we must learn the difference between the two. But it's not enough to stop there; we must take the next step and accept what these sins have done to our lives. The only way to accept this difficult truth is by applying grace. We must accept God's grace in our own lives and extend that grace to others.

If we were perfect people with perfect relationships, we wouldn't need grace. Truth wouldn't be difficult to accept, for it wouldn't contain the wreckage of sinful lives. In a flawed world, however, in order to accept ourselves and others, grace is imperative. Sin constantly binds up relationships with harmful actions, both large and small. Grace allows relationships to flow. Grace untangles the knots of bitterness and blame. With our own sin and the sin of others, there are plenty of both to go around. But where do you get grace, and how do you apply it? The answer is that grace comes from God. Like love and forgiveness, the concept of grace goes against our very nature. Grace is freely given and cannot be earned. It is extended to those who don't deserve it. Although grace is hard to understand, God means for us to have it and experience it. Max Lucado, in his wonderful devotional book, *Experiencing the Heart of Jesus*, says, "Experiencing the grace of Jesus means we feel his strong hand on our shoulders as we hear the words, 'My child, you are free'" (63). Grace brings freedom. The writer of Hebrews, however, warns us that if we miss God's grace, bitterness will grow and cause trouble for many. Without grace, the harsh light of sin can propagate a crop of bitterness and bondage.

Often, just when we've made progress along our healing journey, bypassing the dead end of denial, the root of bitterness trips us up. We're walking along the path of understanding the truth of our past and our situation, sometimes for the first time. The more we dwell on the truth of what was done to us or what we've done to ourselves, the more it hinders us.

Before we know it, we've fed that root of bitterness a steady diet of regret, blame, and shame. It produces a thicket of thorns that bars our forward path to healing. In the midst of the pain of being poked and prodded by angry thorns, denial can suddenly seem like a preferred alternative. If we really understand the truth, it seems as though it leads to more pain. If we stay stuck in denial, we stay stuck. How can we move forward and accept even difficult truths?

Once we truly understand that we are fallen people, living in a fallen world, it can be difficult to accept that God loves us. We know the truth that he does, but we still feel we need to earn it somehow. We think if we can just act better and be better, we can hurdle over regret, blame, and shame on our own. All of this effort is in vain, however. We cannot jump far enough or high enough to get around the consequences of sin. Only God can lift us up through grace. "For by grace you have been saved through faith," Paul said, "and this is not your own doing; it is the gift of God—not the result of works, so that no one may boast" (Ephesians 2:8–9). Grace isn't a right to earn; it's a gift to accept.

Jesus, thank you for your beautiful
gift of grace. May I walk in that
grace today and every day, giving you
glory for your supreme act of love.

✝ ✝ ✝

Each of us must accept God's gift of grace for
ourselves. I've heard grace defined as "unmerited
favor." Some may think this is akin to a free pass. As
such, it's suspect. Where is the fine print? The hidden clauses? If you don't have to do anything to earn
it, then it's free. But if it's free, how is it worth anything? You might be on the right track if grace was
free, but it isn't. Oh, it's free to you and me, but
it came at a tremendous price to God. Listen to
2 Corinthians 8:9: "For you know the generous act
of our Lord Jesus Christ, that though he was rich, yet
for your sakes he became poor, so that by his poverty
you might become rich." This grace, which leads to

our riches, came at the price of Christ's richness. In essence, Jesus has transferred his wealth to us. Do you deserve it? No, and neither do I. Yet God gives it freely anyway as an expression of grace "so that in the ages to come he might show the immeasurable riches of his grace in kindness toward us in Christ Jesus" (Ephesians 2:7). This grace is not about us; it's about God. It's not about who we are; it's about who God is. We are not the focal point of grace; God is. We are merely the recipients.

So what do you do with this grace? How does it allow you to transcend regret, blame, and shame, so you can continue on the healing path? On a personal level, an acceptance of God's grace allows you to put the past behind you. If God has given you grace, how can you refuse to accept it for yourself? "Grace sounds a startling note of contradiction, of liberation," says Phillip Yancey, "and every day I must pray anew for the ability to hear its message" (*What's So Amazing About Grace?*, 71). No matter what your past, no matter what your "poverty," Christ has substituted his riches. You are not a miser before God. Again, when he looks at you, he sees his Son. Whatever sin you've committed in the past is allowed by God to stay there—in the past! You are not meant to drag it along for the rest of your life, slowing you down, tripping you up, fouling your life with shame. By grace, it has been removed from you and placed upon Christ, who has already paid the penalty for that sin. When he said from the cross "It is finished," he meant it.

But grace is much more than just erasing the past; it is about writing the future. When I first met Kary, she wasn't sure the past could ever be erased. Like an after-image burned in her brain, the past swam at the edges of her present. Sexual abuse will do that. Kary felt damaged by her past, with her only option being a scarred future. With nothing to value and hold as worthwhile, she spent her early adulthood in sexual impurity. Introduced to Jesus by a friend, she heard about grace. Without it, she never would have felt "clean" enough to approach God. Experiencing his grace, she understood how she could apply it to her past, her present, and her future.

When you have been given grace, there is an expectation you will live in it. That doesn't just mean sinning freely because you know grace is there to cover you! (The apostle Paul spoke directly against this in Romans 6:1.) Instead, covered with grace, we are to exhibit confidence in our relationship with God himself. The writer of Hebrews said, "Let us

therefore approach the throne of grace with boldness, so that we may receive mercy and find grace to
help in time of need" (Hebrews 4:16). Regret, blame,
and shame, when directed at our own lives, make us
timid or hesitant to approach God. When we understand the truth of who we are in relation to who God
is, it can be overwhelming. By giving us grace, God
invites us to approach him confidently. Grace from
God allows us to enter a *relationship* with him.

✝   ✝   ✝

Teaching Us Grace

When God shows us his grace, he has more in mind
than just our receiving it. He teaches us grace so we
can use it. It is his desire for us to spread that grace
to others. "God is able to make all grace abound to
you," said Paul, "so that in all things at all times,
having all that you need, you will abound in every
good work" (2 Corinthians 9:8, NIV). Freed from the
thicket of regret, blame, and shame, God wants you

to move forward through your life, so you can show grace to others in every situation. It is a paradox that grace cannot be accomplished *by* good works yet it ultimately leads *to* good works. When we try to do "good" works in order to receive grace, our efforts will fail. When grace comes first, good works flow from us as a natural consequence, which God has powered. This, in itself, is an amazing gift!

So how do you act "graciously" toward others, especially among the fallen, who have a tendency to cause pain? The first way is to realize that we all share a common condition—we all need grace. "For by the grace given to me" Paul said, "I say to every-one among you not to think of yourself more highly than you ought to think, but to think with sober judgment, each according to the measure of faith that God has assigned" (Romans 12:3). Those who have been given grace must extend it to others. "But wait," you say, "how can I give grace to someone who treats me badly?" Follow the Romans 12 principle, and ask God to give you discernment about the situation. In other words, was what happened really about you? Are you thinking of yourself more highly than you ought? Sometimes we assume that every-one else acts solely in response to us. We take center stage. A coworker says an unkind word, and we automatically assume it's because he or she is jealous of the job we're doing. Maybe, just maybe, it could be because he or she isn't feeling well or we've taken the comment out of context. When we become upset, we rarely follow up and ask for clarification. Rather, we harbor resentment and anger toward that person, sometimes for years. This is where "sober judgment" comes in—deciding when to just let something go and not take offense.

God, sometimes I focus only on my own pain. Help me open my eyes and see the grace I can give to others.

In the aftermath of trauma and suffering, we can sometimes wear a very thin skin. Any comment or action that has even the appearance of being hurtful is immediately interpreted as a personal attack. Why? Because we haven't fully healed yet. We allow the comment or the action to touch that tender spot, and it hurts! Grace can help with this. Remember, according to the 2 Corinthians verse, grace provides for us in all situations. This doesn't mean you have to pretend that the wounds aren't still raw or partially healed. That wouldn't be the truth. But you can shield those tender spots by allowing grace to cover them, deflecting off what might yet be painful. Grace is the bandage that covers the hurts and allows them to heal. Sometimes, this concept is called giving people "the benefit of the doubt." When you're not absolutely sure that something was meant to harm you, assume it wasn't, and go on from there. If someone means to hurt you, it will become evident in time, and you can confront it when it does.

Growing up, Martin was fat. Other children were unbelievably cruel, and Martin remembers hating school because of the taunts, jokes, and isolation. His peers became his enemies as a child, and he never really did get over that as an adult. The weight came off, after concerted effort, but the defensive mind-set stayed put. He developed an aggressive, reactive approach to any perceived slight, determined never to feel targeted again. His employer finally suggested he get some counseling through the Employee Assistance Program. After a series of sessions, Martin was able to go back to his childhood and extend grace to those childhood memories. He learned to relax around his coworkers and give them the benefit of the doubt. Martin's happier now, and so is everyone else around him!

Our lives, like Martin's, can be filled with casual cruelty. We'd like to be able to lash out and fight back! But Paul said, "Let your speech always be gracious, seasoned with salt, so that you may know how you ought to answer everyone" (Colossians 4:6). Did you notice the last word of this verse, "everyone"? It doesn't say "some people" or "nice people" or "polite people"—it says "everyone," which includes even the person who means to hurt you. Cushioned by grace, we are to respond with gentleness instead of reacting angrily. This implies intentionality, and intentionality is a primary component of grace. Through Christ, God intended to extend us grace, from the beginning of the world. Our sin did not come as a surprise to him. Knowing we would sin, he created us anyway and intentionally set about to bring us back to himself. Sin did not undercut God's plan. Nor should sin undercut our desire to extend grace to others.

With God's help, Grace places us firmly in control of any situation. Again, the 2 Corinthians passage talks about grace "*in all things at all times.*" We've been around long enough to know that all things at all times won't always be pleasant. Grace wouldn't be grace if it covered only those people and situations who didn't need it. And it's no coincidence that God understands grace is given not just with actions but also through words. We inflict pain and injury on others most often through our harsh, unkind, and ungraceful words. James put it this way: "For every species of beast and bird, of reptile and sea creature, can be tamed and has been tamed by the human species, but no one can tame the tongue—a restless evil, full of deadly poison. With it we bless the Lord and Father, and with it we curse those who are made in the likeness of God. From the same mouth come blessing and cursing. My brothers and sisters, this ought not to be so. Does a spring pour forth from the same opening both fresh and brackish water? Can a fig tree, my brothers and sisters, yield olives, or a grapevine figs? No more can salt water yield fresh" (James 3:7–12). Yet God desires our conversations to be full of grace, "seasoned with salt." Some of us have salty speech, but that's not what God is speaking of here!

Think back on those times when others have been verbally abusive or unkind to you. Remember how much that hurt? Our natural inclination would be to give back what we got. Through grace, however, God wants us to give back the good we got from him!

No one said treating others with the grace we've been shown by God is going to be easy. In *What's So Amazing About Grace?*, Phillip Yancey says, "God took a great risk by announcing forgiveness in advance; and the scandal of grace involves a transfer of that risk to us" (180). God understands the risk and difficulty, so he provides us with the grace we need, along with encouragement and hope. "Now may our Lord Jesus Christ himself and God our Father," Paul said, "who loved us and through grace gave us eternal comfort and good hope, comfort your hearts and strengthen them in every good work and word" (2 Thessalonians 2:16–17). The power to act graciously, even to those who do not deserve it, comes directly from Jesus and God. It is God's desire and Christ's example.

Speaking of examples, do you remember the situation with Jim and Steve at the beginning of this chapter? I've seen the same scenario played out in a hundred different families. Over the years, relationships fracture, weighed down by shame and regret. A careless word, a biting comment, a thoughtless action, even a pattern of unloving behaviors or attitudes can be the trigger. It happened in the past, but the hurt remains active in the present and clouds the future. Family members grow up, and some even die—yet the hurt remains. Nobody talks about it openly. Somehow, dealing with sin committed among family members takes on the trappings of a family secret. It's as if the impression of a perfect family is worth denying and ignoring the pain of the past. Each family member needs to be open and ask each other for forgiveness, to extend grace and heal relationships, but no one wants to take the first step. There's a false assumption that when silence covers the issue, it negates the pain.

In many ways, those involved stay stuck in the past, unable to move forward and enjoy each other in the present because of who they were in the past. It's such a waste when a little grace applied to the situation could make all the difference in the world. Most people aren't evil; they're scared, ashamed, selfish, or hurting. They need the balm of grace to heal.

Jim, thinking far too highly of himself, thought he needed to maintain a pretense of maturity and perfection in front of his family. Deep down he was ashamed of how he had treated Steve, but he was afraid of becoming vulnerable if he admitted the truth. Instead, he chose to put his past imperfections behind him, and he wanted Steve to do the same. But every time they got together, he felt awkward, knowing inside that something was left undone. He was unable to find the courage to do it.

Steve didn't realize how much power he really had over the situation. All he knew was that it was just like old times. All along, growing up, feeling tension with Jim was perfectly normal. Steve never felt at ease around Jim. Nor did he know that Jim couldn't relax and just be himself. Perhaps that was what hurt Steve the most. He'd missed out on having a good relationship with his brother growing up. Now, here he was, an adult, and he still couldn't seem to have it. Steve assumed Jim just didn't like him. It made him ashamed that somehow he'd failed as a brother. Whenever they got together, Steve would give Jim a wide berth, assuming his older brother was still upset with him. It never dawned on Steve that Jim was really upset with himself.

Can you relate in some way to this situation? Do you have a strained relationship with a family member? They seem to be at the root of so much hurt in this world. Perhaps nowhere is grace needed more than within the family. For it is within the family that many people feel "safe" to act their worst. They would never think of addressing a friend, colleague, or coworker in the way they talk to a spouse, parent, or sibling. Husbands think they have the right to be served. Wives think they have the right to lash out in anger. Children think they have the right to make demands. Even when people in the family outgrow these positions, many don't take the time to mend the damage, leaving it to fester within their relationships.

This is where grace comes in. God, through grace, re-establishes his relationship with us by granting us what we don't deserve. He loves and forgives us, and he remains faithful to us. He controls the relationship by granting us grace. He doesn't allow our poor performance to bring the relationship down.

Father, grant me the courage and
strength to show grace to those
who have hurt me, especially within
my family.

Can you imagine what would happen if Steve made a decision to relax around Jim? What if he intentionally forgave Jim, put the past behind them, and approached his brother as an adult instead of as that self-centered kid? What if he was to demonstrate his love for Jim by never bringing up the past and, further, by letting it go? Can you imagine what would happen? I can, because I've been privileged to witness families reconciled through grace.

Freed from the shame of his past behavior, Jim would begin to relax around Steve. They'd start calling each other, maybe even getting together more often than just at planned family reunions. At some point, Jim would probably mention to Steve how sorry he was for being such a jerk growing up. Steve would tell him he'd forgiven him and looked forward to a stronger relationship in the future. He might even mention he'd been a bit of a pest himself!

I've seen it happen in situations like this. And I've seen grace applied to appalling situations where grievous hurt has taken place, with the kind of behavior you couldn't imagine anyone ever being forgiven for. Yet, even there, grace was applied. Why? Because the person who applied the grace had received it from God and felt compelled to spread that grace *in all things at all times*, even things and times that would seem impossible to us. But Jesus himself said that with God, all things are possible (see Mark 10:27). And he should know. John Trent reminds us in *Choosing to Live the Blessing*, "The choices we make to bless or curse others are also being watched" (4). Grace finds the strength to bless when cursing seems the right response.

Grace and Truth

The apostle John said Jesus came with both truth and grace (see John 1:14, 17). They go together. Our truth is that we desperately need grace. God's truth is that he willingly provides it. On your path to healing, you begin with truth and continue on by accepting grace. For it is only through grace that you are able to *experience* forgiveness. And it is only through grace that you are able to *extend* forgiveness. So by accepting God's grace, you will continue on the path to healing.

Chapter Three

Forgiveness

I Will Let Go and Let God Lead Me to Forgiveness

Hopefully, you've detected a pattern—a map, if you will—for this healing journey. You start with truth and continue on to acceptance of grace. It is important to keep going because one of your most important destinations is just ahead: forgiveness. Once you know and understand the truth of the damage of sin, it is impossible to arrive at forgiveness without grace. Grace allows us to bridge the gap between truth and forgiveness.

Why is forgiveness a desired destination? It is the place where you experience freedom from the burden of your own sins and from bondage to the sins of others. Without that freedom, you will continue to carry anger, guilt, fear, shame, and blame. These unwelcome companions will weigh you down, wear you out, and weaken your resolve to keep moving forward to healing.

Julie remembered with vivid clarity the day she became her mother. Up to that time, she'd made it a point to act differently from her mother—to live a better life and to never give her mother an excuse for her bad behavior. Growing up, Julie endured an endless stream of harsh remarks and criticism. Her mother, however, had an equally inexhaustible supply of excuses for her own behavior. The world was against her mother, and Julie was supposed to understand when her mother was short-tempered, moody, pessimistic, or preoccupied. Julie learned to say nothing, to make no protests on her own behalf, and to swallow her anger and bow her head against her mother's rage. It was the only way to survive.

Survival meant staying underneath her mother's radar. And as long as her rage was directed at something or someone else, Julie was safe. But inside, she vibrated with a rage of her own that manifested itself in a cold and distant relationship with her mother. Julie did not, would not, forgive her.

Then, it happened. Julie's daughter, who had been potty training for the past week, had an accident. Well, not an accident really. Julie was sure that her daughter, McKenna, knew she needed to go to the bathroom but chose to stay seated on the couch so she could finish watching cartoons. It didn't matter that she wasn't yet two years old. All that mattered was a stressful day, soiled pants, and a stained couch. Before she knew what she was doing, Julie yelled at her daughter, jerked her up from the couch, and set her hard upon the toilet. There was no mistaking her displeasure, and McKenna responded by crying at the top of her lungs. Julie looked at her daughter and felt satisfaction at her distress— and in that moment, she became her mother.

The Freedom to Forgive Others

We live in a fallen world among people who will hurt us and cause us pain both intentionally and unintentionally. Nancy Guthrie put it this way: "Death, disease, destruction—these are all the result of living in a world where sin has taken root and corrupted everything" (*Holding on to Hope*, 31). This can lead to a sort of bondage; we are enmeshed within the pain caused by sin while struggling against it and becoming more and more tightly bound to it. Somehow, we have to find a way to break free and live unencumbered. God has shown us the way through his example of forgiveness.

Hear and Forgive

In the Old Testament books of 1 Kings and 2 Chronicles, God gives us the "hear and forgive" example of his forgiveness. This is an easy example for us to identify with, for it involves hearing the plea for forgiveness and then granting it. In these two books, the people of Israel called out to God, who heard them from heaven and forgave their sin (1 Kings 8:30, 34, 36, 39; 2 Chronicles 6:21, 25, 27, 30, 39). Forgiveness follows a plea for the same. It makes sense to us that if someone does us wrong, that person should recognize it and ask for our forgiveness.

Some of us desire nothing more than for the one who wronged us to cry out for our forgiveness. We dream of being in the position of 2 Chronicles 7:14: "If my people who are called by my name humble themselves, pray, seek my face, and turn from their wicked ways, then I will hear from heaven, and will forgive their sin and heal their land." We want the person to acknowledge a relationship with us ("if my people who are called by my name"), exhibit an attitude of submission to us ("humble themselves, pray, seek my face"), and show their remorse ("and turn from their wicked ways"). If all these conditions are met, then we will consider forgiving.

God, of course, restores the relationship broken by sin ("then I will hear from heaven"), agrees to the request ("and will forgive their sin"), and goes even further to provide blessings ("and heal their land"). That is what God does, but it doesn't always work that way with us. Even if the person does all of the above, we may still withhold forgiveness because of the depth of our own hurt. We may not have the freedom of forgiveness, but we'll gladly settle for the satisfaction of their humiliation. The truth is, their humiliation is what we desire most. Through it, we feel vindicated and powerful, especially if their sin against us made us feel powerless, vulnerable, and victimized. We want them to beg for forgiveness in order to exact revenge. We want to dangle the carrot of forgiveness in front of them in order to wield the stick of retribution.

This is not the purpose of forgiveness. For example, God does not need to forgive us in order to feel powerful; he is almighty. It is not being in the position to forgive that exhibits power but the expression of forgiveness that proves it. The psalmist said, "But with you there is forgiveness; therefore you are feared" (Psalm 130:4, NIV). It doesn't say that God is feared because he *might* forgive; it says he is feared because he *does* forgive. The act of forgiveness is the sovereign act. It is not a submissive act; it is an act of power.

Father, when others hurt me, I want to hurt them back. Grant me the courage to look to you for comfort, so I can truly forgive.

Our Model of Forgiveness

God doesn't kid around when it comes to forgiveness. He doesn't take it lightly, and he doesn't consider it optional. On the contrary, forgiveness is so important that he sent his son to die to obtain forgiveness for us from God, and God holds us accountable to also be forgiving. Consider Matthew 6:12 and Luke 11:4, both passages from the Scriptures known as the Lord's Prayer. Both verses link the forgiveness we receive from God to the forgiveness we extend to others: "And forgive us our debts, as we also have forgiven our debtors" (Matthew 6:12); and "And forgive us our sins, for we ourselves forgive everyone indebted to us" (Luke 11:4). Matthew went on to reiterate the point: "For if you forgive others their trespasses, your heavenly Father will also forgive you; but if you do not forgive others, neither will your Father forgive your trespasses" (Matthew 6:14–15). In this way, we become the model God uses for our own forgiveness. Put another way, God lets us know that if we insist upon choosing a different model of forgiveness than Christ's, then we can no longer receive God's forgiveness.

This debt of forgiveness can give us difficulty. Andy had trouble with forgiveness, especially when it came to his coworker, Brian. They used to be good friends at work until Brian passed along a comment Andy made about their boss. It wound up as part of Andy's annual review. Brian had apologized, but Andy knew it was a way for Brian to look better in the eyes of their supervisor. Why should he forgive Brian when Brian had done it deliberately? It wasn't just about friendship anymore, it was about a paycheck. Brian could ask for forgiveness, and Andy could even say it was no big deal. But it was, and Andy wasn't about to forget it.

It doesn't seem right or fair that we should have to forgive other people who sin against us in order for God to forgive us. What does one have to do with the other? And shouldn't there be a limit on how much we're expected to forgive someone else? This last question even came up among the disciples of Christ. After Peter listened to Jesus speak on how to handle someone who sins against us, Peter asked, "Lord, if another member of the church sins against me, how often should I forgive? As many as seven times?" (Matthew 18:21). *Seven times? That's quite a bit*, Peter may have been thinking. *Jesus will probably be quite impressed with my understanding of forgiveness.* Most of us would question whether or not to trust someone who sinned against us seven times. Jesus' answer, however, is startling. He said that we are to forgive "Not seven times, but, I tell you, seventy-seven times" (Matthew 18:22). Seventy-seven times over? There's obviously a different principle at stake here!

† † †

God's Model of Forgiveness

Anticipating Peter's reaction, Jesus went on to explain this seemingly outrageous answer in the parable of the unforgiving servant. Instead of paraphrasing it, I'll let you listen to Jesus tell the story: "For this reason the kingdom of heaven may be

compared to a king who wished to settle accounts
with his slaves. When he began the reckoning, one
who owed him ten thousand talents [a talent was
worth more than 15 years of a laborer's wages] was
brought to him; and, as he could not pay, his lord
ordered him to be sold, together with his wife and
children and all his possessions, and payment to be
made. So the slave fell on his knees before him,
saying, 'Have patience with me, and I will pay you
everything.' And out of pity for him, the lord of
that slave released him and forgave him the debt.
But that same slave, as he went out, came upon
one of his fellow-slaves who owed him a hundred
denarii [the denarius was the usual day's wage for a
laborer]; and seizing him by the throat, he said, 'Pay
what you owe.' Then his fellow-slave fell down and
pleaded with him, 'Have patience with me, and I will
pay you.' But he refused; then he went and threw
him into prison until he should pay the debt. When
his fellow-slaves saw what had happened, they were
greatly distressed, and they went and reported to
their lord all that had taken place. Then his lord
summoned him and said to him, 'You wicked slave!
I forgave you all that debt because you pleaded with
me. Should you not have had mercy on your fellow-

slave, as I had mercy on you?' And in anger his lord handed him over to be tortured until he should pay his entire debt. So my heavenly Father will also do to every one of you, if you do not forgive your brother or sister from your heart" (Matthew 18:23–35).

To me, it's the last phrase of this story that holds its power: "from your heart." God expects a *heart change* to occur when we forgive others. Listen to the words of Drs. Les and Leslie Parrott in their book, *Relationships*: "Our primal urge of 'balancing the score' comes to a screeching halt when we set our pride aside and begin to forgive" (100). This heart change transforms us and, hopefully, transforms the person we've forgiven. At the very least, we experience transformation even if the other person does not. So much of forgiveness has little to do with the other person and more to do with us.

Christ's Model of Forgiveness

Again, it can seem to us as if forgiveness means letting someone who has wronged us "off the hook." If someone asks for forgiveness, we're supposed to give it: "If another disciple sins, you must rebuke the offender, and if there is repentance, you must forgive" (Luke 17:3). We're even supposed to be proactive with forgiveness and just do it: "Bear with one another and, if anyone has a complaint against another, forgive each other; just as the Lord has forgiven you, so you also must forgive" (Colossians 3:13). "Where is justice?" we ask. God provides the answer in Hebrews 9:22 when he reminds us, "without the shedding of blood there is no forgiveness of sins." Justice demands that those sins be accounted for—and they are—through Christ.

Jesus, thank you for giving your-

self as a sacrifice for my sins.

Without your gift, I was lost; with

your gift, I am whole.

✝   ✝   ✝

As we ponder the personal implications of forgiveness, each of us should take time to reflect upon the
sacrifice of Jesus, foretold in the Book of Isaiah: "But
he was wounded for our transgressions, crushed for
our iniquities; upon him was the punishment that
made us whole, and by his bruises we are healed"
(Isaiah 53:5). We contemplate Christ's death on the
cross and feel overwhelming gratitude and amaze-
ment at the love he had for us—to willingly go
through that horrible death to forgive our sins. We
understand that Christ suffered for our forgiveness,
but perhaps we should go a bit further.

Read the next verse in Isaiah: "All we like sheep have gone astray; we have all turned to our own way, and the Lord has laid on him the iniquity of us all" (Isaiah 53:6). Do you understand what that means? It means that God has laid on Christ not only the sins you commit but also the sins others have committed *against* you. When you feel that the wrongs done to you should be paid for, remember that they have been, by Christ. And when you withhold from someone the forgiveness they ask for, you say to Christ, *No, you will not carry that sin. The person who wronged me must carry the Cross for their own sin.* To which God replies, *If you insist that person carry their own Cross, then you must carry your own.*

I don't know about you, but I can't carry my own sin. So if I want God to forgive me, I have no choice but to forgive others. Or do I? The choice may lie not in whether I forgive but in whether *I trust.* It is an act of faith to forgive the sins committed against me. For I am saying to the person, *Knowing that you have the power to hurt me, I choose to remain in a relationship with you.* I am saying to God, "I trust you to protect me, and I trust you to teach me." In *The Peacemaker,* Ken Sande says, "When you perceive that the person who has wronged you is being used as an instrument in God's hand to help you mature, serve others, and glorify him, it may be easier for you to move ahead with forgiveness" (195). When we put our trust in God and obediently forgive, we experience freedom from fear, worry, and doubt. God is able to use even the most painful situations for our good.

For some of you, a question may still linger: "What about the really bad people who don't want forgiveness?" The truth is that Christ paid the price for their sins, too. The tragedy for them is that they reject his gift. The benefits of forgiveness cannot be experienced by those who don't want it and refuse to accept it. Oh, forgiveness can be given—your forgiveness, Christ's forgiveness—but the benefits of a restored relationship with you and with God are not possible without repentance. Forgiveness on your part allows you to move past the sin committed against you. Repentance on their part allows a restored relationship. If the person does not repent, the relationship stays fractured, and you will have to move on without a restoration. Moving on may mean leaving the unrepentant behind. Sometimes, people are repentant, but they are too ashamed or proud to verbalize their repentance. Instead, they slowly alter their behavior without articulating the need for your forgiveness. When this happens, the relationship has a good chance of being restored, though it usually takes longer and requires more trust on your part.

When Julie realized she was capable of treating her own daughter the same way she'd been treated, it came as a revelation. At first, it terrified her to think she was capable of the same type of behavior. I explained to her that no one is immune from feelings of frustration, anger, and resentment. Rather, it is what we do with those feelings that make the difference. Julie's mother chose to place responsibility for those feelings on others, blaming them for her own negative emotions. In contrast, Julie—realizing how harsh she'd been with her daughter—immediately apologized and comforted McKenna. It did, however, open up a window into her mother's behavior Julie had never seen before. This tiny crack allowed Julie to take a small step on the path toward forgiveness. In time, she came to understand that her mother was a broken, bitter woman whose desperate, controlling need for love suffocated others and left little room to respond in kind. Within God's carefully considered boundaries, Julie has forgiven her mother. Within prayerfully considered boundaries, Julie has reintroduced a relationship with her mother. Without the first, the second would not have been possible.

† † †

The Freedom to Forgive Yourself

It is quite true that often the person we have the hardest time forgiving is ourselves. We may have successfully forgiven others but still feel trapped in our own self-condemnation. But if God expects you to honor the repentance of others by granting them forgiveness, do you think he's going to allow you to beat yourself up even though you experience remorse and repentance yourself? If he died for the sins of the world, why do you think he would allow you to hold back your own sins for special punishment? How is your self-flagellation going to improve upon the sacrifice of Christ? Is your solution to your sin better than his? This is not humility; it is arrogance. You are putting yourself—your desires, your need for self-punishment, your sin solution—above God.

Again, it comes down to an issue of trust. Do you trust God to love you and forgive you? Repeat these verses in Psalm 103 and personalize them: "Bless the Lord, O my soul, and do not forget all his benefits—who forgives all [my] iniquity…who redeems [my] life from the Pit, who crowns [me] with steadfast love and mercy…. The Lord is merciful and gracious, slow to anger and abounding in steadfast love. He will not always accuse, nor will he keep his anger for ever. He does not deal with [me] according to [my] sins, nor repay [me] according to [my] iniquities. For as the heavens are high above the earth, so great is his steadfast love [for me]; as far as the east is from the west, so far he removes [my] transgressions from [me]" (Psalm 103:2–4; 8–12). It all comes down to whether you believe God or not. If you believe him, then those sins you want to hold back are already forgiven because of his love for you. Let them go! They have been paid for; you are redeemed!

Father, I release my sins to you;
I accept your forgiveness. Free me
from this shame and release my
heart from guilt.

✝   ✝   ✝

When you understand and acknowledge your own
sinfulness, it's easier for you to depersonalize the sins
of others, recognizing it's not about you; it's about *sin*.
This allows for relationships to flow more smoothly.
After all, the whole point of forgiveness is restoration
of relationships—God's with us and ours with other
people. We need God, and we need each other. He
calls us to be a *family*, united in love with each other,
bearing with one another. Remember the Colossians
passage? "Bear with one another and, if anyone has a
complaint against another, forgive each other; just as
the Lord has forgiven you, so you also must forgive"

(Colossians 3:13). This is embedded within a beautiful passage on how to live together in peace.

Peaceful living—and forward momentum on the path to healing—requires that you accept God's forgiveness of your own sins so you can move on, unburdened. It demands that you extend your own forgiveness to others so you can restore as many relationships as possible. Forgiveness is an imperative, not an option bestowed only when you feel like giving it to others or granted only when you feel like you deserve it yourself. And if you still struggle with how to forgive, I encourage you to read the Gospel accounts of the betrayal, trial, and crucifixion of Christ. See how he handled the slander of leaders, the abandonment and betrayal of close friends, the mocking of the crowds, the physical beatings, and the long climb to the Cross. Meditate on all he suffered and how he was able at the end to pray to God for forgiveness for those who pierced and crushed and wounded him, all within the context of his total innocence.

Then realize his prayer of forgiveness can be yours as well.

Chapter Four

Gratitude

*I Will Let Go and Let God
Inspire My Joy*

As you continue on your healing journey past the
point of forgiveness, you leave behind anger, fear,
guilt, blame, and shame. But the spaces where
those negative emotions used to reside can
remain empty. It's not enough to let go of that
negativity; you need to fill yourself up with positive feelings. And you don't just want to fill
yourself up; you want to stuff yourself as Jesus
described in his teaching about giving and
receiving: "A good measure, pressed down,
shaken together, *running over...*" (Luke 6:38,

emphasis added). And one of the most positive attitudes you can stuff yourself with is gratitude. Press yourself down with gratitude, and you'll find yourself running over with joy.

Gratitude and forgiveness spring forth from the same place—the heart. You saw in the last chapter how forgiveness is a heart-change. Gratitude is a heart-*state* according to Colossians 3:16. This state-of-heart can protect you from being overrun again by those negative emotions. Jesus explained this principle when he talked about a man who got rid of an "unclean spirit" (Matthew 12:43–45). With this spirit gone, the man leaves the space empty, swept, and in order. Yet the unclean spirit decides to return to the man, and when it finds the space cleared out, but unoccupied, it sets up residence again along with seven others "more evil than itself." Jesus went on to say that the man is now far worse off than he was at first. It is not enough to rid yourself of anger, fear, guilt, blame, and shame; you must replace them with joy, confidence, peace, mercy, and godly pride. God is able to provide each of these in flowing abundance in your life.

Mark's marriage ended badly. He fought it, kicking and screaming, until his wife made it quite clear she no longer wanted anything to do with him. She was done with him and the marriage. It didn't matter how much he still loved her; she no longer loved him. She couldn't even stand to be anywhere near him. There was someone else, and she wanted that relationship more than she wanted him. She was finished, and for a time, Mark thought he was, too. Nothing made sense anymore. He couldn't understand what he'd done wrong or why someone who had loved him once could come to hate him so much. Had she ever really loved him at all? How could he have been so blind?

For a long time after the divorce, he didn't want to see anyone. His friends had been their friends, and some were now only her friends. With a morbid fascination, he tried to keep up with what she was doing. That ended when he found out she'd married again. She was moving on with her life, and Mark couldn't seem to get on with his. What right did she have to be happy when she'd made him absolutely miserable? It wasn't fair.

A good friend finally took him aside and told him it was time to let his ex-wife go. All of the time they were married, he had held on to her out of love. Since the divorce, he had held on to her out of anger. He needed to let her go—to let the anger go. It was like a breath of fresh air sweeping over his heart when he found the strength to forgive her and move on. He decided he was not going to concentrate on those last ten months but on the five years before that when he'd been happy. He realized he was grateful to her for helping him develop an understanding of love. Ultimately, she threw it away, but Mark found he was ready to reclaim it. With this renewed confidence in his ability to give and receive love, Mark was ready to put the past behind him and embrace the future.

How do you pass from pain to joy? How can you be grateful, especially for those events in life when you are deeply wounded? In *Holding on to Hope*, Nancy Guthrie asks an important question: "Would you be willing to thank God for a gift he gave you and has now taken away?" (27). For most of us, our natural inclination, when we lose something or are in pain, is to lash out and fight back or cower against the pain and pull into ourselves. Joy is not our first reaction. Yet James said it should be: "My brothers and sisters, whenever you face trials of any kind, consider it nothing but joy, because you know that the testing of your faith produces endurance" (James 1:2–3). Gratitude is not our natural response to pain. Yet Paul said we should give thanks for everything (Ephesians 5:20) and in all circumstances (1 Thessalonians 5:18).

"Now, wait," you say, "surely there are exceptions! How could God expect me to be thankful for everything? I'm not supposed to be thankful for bad things that happen to me!" There are two reactions when something bad happens to you—you can be upset and angry or you can look to God to provide you with direction, understanding, and context. Within the latter, gratitude—even for the bad things—is possible.

Still not convinced? You need look no further than the Last Supper. Jesus spent the evening in the midst of a group of his dearest friends on earth, one of whom would betray him, all of whom would desert him. Through the breaking of the bread and pouring of the wine, he gave witness to his death, knowing it was fast approaching. And what did he do before he presented the bread as his body and the wine as his blood? He gave *thanks* to God. Jesus knew he was going to encounter a very bad thing—death on a cross—but with God's direction and understanding, he was able to give thanks, even before it happened! God's direction and understanding can allow you to do the same. You can fill up those hurt places with gratitude and joy!

Lord, I give you my anger and pain. I ask you to turn them into gratitude and joy. This is much bigger than me; I cannot do it without you.

Let Joy Take the Place of Anger

Anger can be a difficult emotion to let go. Sharon sure wanted to hold on to hers. Growing up, her father was an alcoholic who drifted in and out of her life. He drifted in when he needed something, and she prayed for him to drift out whenever he was drunk. She came to hate him even as she yearned for him to love her. As she grew up, Sharon took that longing and stuck it someplace far from her heart, so it couldn't hurt her again. But when news came that her father, now old, was dying, she wasn't sure she wanted to see him, even though he'd asked for her. She went to see him only to realize he just wanted someone to take care of him while he died. As usual, it wasn't about anyone else but him. The urge to strike back against him in anger was almost overwhelming.

Anger makes you feel empowered, vindicated, and strong. It sustains you and gives your life an absorbing purpose. Full-blown anger fills up every space and leaves no room for despair and reflection. Anger presses outward and provides a barricade against vulnerability. Anger can transport you from a valley of pain to a mountaintop of rage. Because it is exceedingly powerful, we want to hang on to it. We feel we *need* to hang on to it. Sharon had hung on to hers so long that she wasn't sure she could let go of it. It dawned on her, however, that her anger had become her idol. She was worshiping and tending to her anger instead of God.

If you stand before the altar of anger, God says you can't stand in front of his. "But I say to you that if you are angry with a brother or sister, you will be liable to judgment; and if you insult a brother or sister, you will be liable to the council; and if you say, 'You fool,' you will be liable to the hell of fire. So when you are offering your gift at the altar, if you remember that your brother or sister has something against you, leave your gift there before the altar and go; first be reconciled to your brother or sister, and then come and offer your gift" (Matthew 5:22–24). If you are angry and don't reconcile that anger, you have unfinished business that will interfere with your relationship with God.

Because anger is powerful, God tells us to be extremely careful with it, for it can be all-consuming and even self-consuming. "Let everyone be quick to listen, slow to speak, slow to anger; for your anger does not produce God's righteousness" (James 1:19–20). Rather than be filled with anger, God wants us to be empowered with joy, which is also all-consuming, powerful, and transporting. Anger drags us down while joy lifts us up. We could feel angry when troubles befall us, but instead God wants us to be filled with joy because the context of that joy is an ever-increasing, resilient faith. James went on to say that we have joy in trials because we know that this testing of our faith produces endurance: "And let endurance have its full effect, so that you may be mature and complete, lacking in nothing" (James 1:4). Lacking in nothing: that is, not lacking in thankfulness and not lacking in joy.

Sharon almost missed out. Her anger almost kept her from the last seven months of her dad's life. As he became frail, his demeanor changed; he went from brusque to remorseful. It was as if the cancer was eating away not only at his organs but also at all the barriers he'd erected to cope with his life. He began to appreciate Sharon's presence. He learned to cry out for her in his pain. Freed from his addiction to alcohol, he was able to express his love for her. She'd never have experienced his love if she'd rejected him as he lay dying. Anger kept her strong; forgiveness kept her vulnerable. Vulnerable, she was able to heal. Sharon now looks back on those seven months as the most difficult yet rewarding time of her life.

† † †

Let Confidence Take the Place of Fear

Fear is a common human reaction. In fact, fear of God is called the beginning of knowledge (Proverbs 1:7). So fear is not always a bad thing. But on the path to recovery, fear of the unknown, fear of being hurt again, and fear of our standing before God can keep us stuck. "Fear can keep us bound so that we live less and less of life. The cost is the life that we did not live because of the fear," say Henry Cloud and John Townsend in *God Will Make a Way* (187). God wants our fear to be based on an understanding of him and his power. We are right to fear God, but he doesn't want us to stay stuck there. God wants us to move away from fear to confidence in Christ.

The writer of Hebrews said, "So we can say with confidence, 'The Lord is my helper; I will not be afraid. What can anyone do to me?'" (Hebrews 13:6). You may answer, "Well, they can do a lot!" And that is very true, but the basis of our confidence comes in the Lord as our helper. We are not alone; we are not undefended; we are not without a champion. We can move beyond fear—we can be unafraid because our confidence is in the Lord.

Listen to 2 Corinthians 3:4–5: "Such is the confidence that we have through Christ towards God. Not that we are competent of ourselves to claim anything as coming from us; our competence is from God." As we heal from trauma, there can be so much to fear—that what happened before will happen again, that we won't be strong enough to break beyond the past, and that we'll never be able to truly be happy again. All of these fears cause our steps to be unsteady, hesitant, and faltering. While we cannot always trust

ourselves, we can always trust God. Our confidence
and competence to go forward comes from him.

Why should God provide us with this confidence?
Because of Jesus! Paul explained it this way: "This
was in accordance with the eternal purpose that he
has carried out in Christ Jesus our Lord, in whom
we have access to God in boldness and confidence
through faith in him" (Ephesians 3:11–12). Boldness
and confidence—no more bondage and fear!

Jesus, help me be bold and have
confidence to approach the Father
because of what you have done
and not who I am.

Let Peace Take the Place of Guilt

Guilt is a crushing load that breaks the back of even a very strong person. No one can bear up under such a load. This is why God in his mercy took away our guilt and substituted peace through Christ (Romans 5:1), for few things rob us of peace more than our own guilt. We feel obliged to pick it up and carry it around with us wherever we go. It can feel odd and unnatural to leave it behind. Guilt, therefore, is a prime candidate for sneaking its way back into our lives if we don't replace it with peace.

Not all guilt is wrong, of course. God gave us a conscience, an internal radar of right and wrong, as explained in the first chapter of Romans. Godly remorse is an appropriate response to our own sin. Guilt, however, has a way of appearing, uninvited, from bogus sources. Other people may have demanded that you carry their guilt for events that happened in your past. Persuasive, they convinced you that the guilt with their name on it should rightly be shouldered by you. Or you may have assumed that since you were carrying around a load of guilt of your own making, it was appropriate for others to add more guilt to the pile. Already guilty, you felt powerless to object. If this is how you've felt, please remember that in John 14:27, Jesus said he came not to judge the world (to add to your guilt) but to save it (to remove your guilt). "Contrary to popular opinion," says Chuck Swindoll, "God doesn't sit in heaven with His jaws clenched, His arms folded in disapproval, and a deep frown on His brow" (*Hope Again*, 65). Through Christ, you have peace with God, peace with others, and peace with yourself.

This peace of Christ was such a reality to the first Christians, they used it as a greeting and a salutation—a way of saying hello and goodbye. This is especially true of Paul, who was "guilty" of having persecuted Christ himself. If Paul could lay down that guilt and find peace, so can you! Listen to Paul in 2 Thessalonians 3:16: "Now may the Lord of peace himself give you peace at all times in all ways. The Lord be with all of you." Peace at all times and in all ways: This is the gift of God through Christ when our guilt is removed.

One of the most beautiful greetings in the Bible comes from Numbers 6:24–26: "The Lord bless you and keep you; the Lord make his face to shine upon you, and be gracious to you; the Lord lift up his countenance upon you, and give you peace." This is God's desire for you—to bless you and keep you, to shine his face upon you, to be gracious to you, and to give you peace. Why? Because he loves you.

† † †

Let Mercy Take the Place of Blame

Some of us operate as if forgiveness has a quota. In other words, if we feel as though we've forgiven people for a lot in the past, it becomes harder for us to forgive in the future. Because we've had to suffer at the hands of others, we feel justified in a harsh attitude toward others if we feel they've wronged us.

Again, we develop a "thin skin" where any hurt is involved.

As a child, Jan's father abused her, and she used this abuse to justify her habit of treating all of the men she met with suspicion and hostility. As hard as it was for those men she worked with, it was even worse for her husband. Any imperfection, anything out of line, and he got blasted with the reservoir of Jan's anger from the past. Double-barrel blasts. His protests that he wasn't the one who had abused her was met with her recitation of all of the ways he had wronged her in the past. She painted them with the same brush as her father's abuse. It got so tangled that when they argued, he never could seem to find a way out unscathed. Physically abused by her father, Jan emotionally abused her husband. She kept thinking her anger would make her feel better, but it didn't.

We are not allowed to transfer the pain we feel over one person's wrong to another. Was it wrong for Jan's father to abuse her? Yes, but it is also wrong of her to transfer that blame onto someone else. Forgiveness means removing that pain from adversely affecting your attitude and behavior. With the pain removed, the desire to blame is deflated.

Frankly, if we were to spend our time focusing on how others hurt us, it would become a full-time job. People, being people, let us down, are careless in word and deed, and neglect our needs for their own. This is why it is vital for us to remember that we do the very same thing. If we insist upon blaming others, they have a tendency to find reasons to blame us right back. This is a cycle of unforgiveness that binds up relationships and leads to bitterness. The only balm for this bitterness and blame is mercy.

Jesus certainly had reason to be bitter. Being blameless, he bore the penalty for our sin. He understood that mercy is a necessity when dealing with sinners. "Go and learn what this means, 'I desire mercy, not sacrifice.' For I have come to call not the righteous but sinners" (Matthew 9:13). God desires mercy from us also. Just as with forgiveness, those of us who expect to receive mercy must extend it. James was quite clear on this point: "For judgment will be without mercy to anyone who has shown no mercy; mercy triumphs over judgment" (James 2:13). And mercy triumphs over blame!

Let Pride Take the Place of Shame

Acknowledging our sin can produce a harvest of shame. While God wants us to understand and appreciate the reality of sin, we are not meant to live a life burdened with shame. Instead, God wants us to live a victorious life, a "pride full" life. The Old Testament is full of this concept of "pride." It is shown as a two-edged sword, however. Those who take pride in themselves and their own accomplishments are destined for a "fall," as in Proverbs 16:18: "Pride goes before destruction, and a haughty spirit before a fall." Does this mean we are to walk around, head bowed, and ashamed? No!

We take pride in the accomplishments of others (2 Corinthians 7:4; 8:24). We can even take appropriate pride in our own accomplishments with a qualification: "Each one should test his own actions. Then he can take pride in himself, without comparing himself to somebody else" (Galatians 6:4 NIV).

Those who wallow in blame desire to see you clothed in shame. For when you are ashamed, you are vulnerable to their needs and desires. Shame is a way to control you. God, however, turns these weaknesses—these "shameful" things—and uses them for his glory. Just as Jesus said he didn't come to heal the healthy but the sick (Matthew 9:12; Mark 2:17; Luke 5:31), God uses our weaknesses to display his strength and power.

Paul learned this truth from the Lord and gave us the concept in 2 Corinthians 12:9: "But he said to me, 'My grace is sufficient for you, for power is made perfect in weakness.' So, I will boast all the more gladly of my weaknesses, so that the power of Christ may dwell in me." Do you understand what this means? All of those things you've been ashamed of, you can now boast about! Why? Because God has taken you and your shameful things and is moving you toward healing! Your healing gives testimony to the world of his power to change lives! So go ahead and boast! Boast about God's transforming power in your life. Take pride in your new life in Christ: "In order that, as it is written, 'Let the one who boasts, boast in the Lord'" (1 Corinthians 1:31).

Fill Yourself Up With Good Things

The pain of this world can produce so much that is negative, but God is able to take those negatives and turn them into positives. As you consider more ways to fill yourself up with good things, don't forget Galatians 5:22–23: "By contrast, the fruit of the Spirit is love, joy, peace, patience, kindness, generosity, faithfulness, gentleness, and self-control. There is no law against such things." So go ahead and let yourself be filled! Ask God to help you clean out the old, negative spaces, so you'll have room for the renewing attributes of a healed, redeemed life.

Chapter Five

Transformation

I Will Let Go and Let God Transform Me

In a fallen world, the path to healing can be long. Therefore, perseverance and stamina are essential. Because anger, fear, guilt, blame, and shame drain us and make our life seem dark, exhausting, and fraught with problems, it is vital for us to remember that while we are on the path to healing, our minds show us the way, but our spirit energizes us, and our bodies get us there. Negative emotions sap us of our mental and physical strength, but the opposite is also true: Positive emotions invigorate us, giving us the boost we need to continue on through difficult stretches.

Grief crept up on Pam in the middle of a sunny afternoon, with flowers all around. Staying inside just wasn't an option on such a beautiful day, so she'd gone out in the backyard to weed. As she worked her way through the warm, damp beds, she came upon the calla lilies. Peeking up through the broad green leaves was the first blossom. Grief slammed down hard as Pam remembered this was her father's plant. He'd painstakingly transported it from family home to family home across three states. When she'd moved into her first house, her father's calla lily went with her.

She sat back on her heels, tears springing to her eyes. It wasn't fair that her father was dead;

he was too young. It wasn't his time to go. He should have taken better care of himself. Look at all she and her family missed because of his death. Her children would grow up without knowing their grandfather. No more holiday celebrations. No more vacations to see grandma *and* grandpa. No high school graduations. No sharing college plans. No weddings. No great-grandchildren. The only interaction left for her children was with a memory, fast fading as they grew up, and pictures in frames on the piano in the living room. Not a living, breathing, laughing, loving grandfather. Anger welled up inside her, causing even more tears. It just wasn't right. It just wasn't fair.

"Stop," she told herself firmly. "It's not his fault he's dead. It's not God's fault either." Pam's father had died of congestive heart failure after a series of heart attacks, beginning when she'd still been in school and living at home. He'd done what he could to moderate the damage—he lost weight, quit smoking, and became more active. The damage was done, though, and it eventually caught up to him. "Don't dwell on his death," she told herself, gently working the weeds away from the base of the plant. "Concentrate on his life!" As soon as her daughter got home from school, Pam took her out in the yard, showed her the beautiful new blossom coming up, and reminded her about her grandfather.

We've talked about the importance of gratitude and joy in our lives. As we walk this path toward healing, we should take as many positive companions with us as we can. The negative ones seem to come along uninvited. The positive ones we must make a conscious effort to include. Let's take a look again at the Letter to the Galatians and that wonderful list of positive companions, also known as "the fruit of the Spirit." To review, they are given as "…love, joy, peace, patience, kindness, generosity, faithfulness, gentleness, and self-control" (Galatians 5:22–23).

Holy Spirit, be with me as I heal.
Let your good fruit crowd out the
weeds of bitterness and anger.
Transform my mind to think your
thoughts and not my own.

Love

We have talked about how it can be difficult to love others, even ourselves, in the midst of pain. Again, let me emphasize that through God's power we *can* love. John reminds us, "We love because he first loved us" (1 John 4:19). We are not the originators of love; God is. It is his love we receive and reflect. When you feel your ability to love compromised by the suffering and hardships you've been through, remember that God is willing and able to open up your heart to his love. This comes from seeing the world through God's eyes. This comes from experiencing God's heart.

Joy

Joy springs forth from an understanding of who God is and how much he loves you. When you feel your strength flagging on your healing path, a great way to reclaim your joy is to remind yourself of how much God loves you. And by anchoring your joy to the bedrock of God's character, you can be assured that you will find your way back, no matter what.

Peace

Just as Jesus was ready to depart from this world and return to his Father, he gave us this promise: "Peace I leave with you; my peace I give to you. I do not give to you as the world gives. Do not let your hearts be troubled, and do not let them be afraid" (John 14:27). Jesus knew how elusive peace in this world can be, so he made sure we have no misunderstandings about how we are to find peace. And it's not just any peace, or worldly peace, but *his* peace. We must substitute our own efforts to find peace through the things of this world or the logic of this world and look instead to the peace of Jesus. Max Lucado points out, "We must realize all we are doing to produce lasting peace in our own strength is not working" (*Experiencing the Heart of Jesus*, 38). Our own strength to produce peace in our lives is inadequate; God's peace is infinite and available: "And the peace of God, which surpasses all understanding, will guard your hearts and your minds in Christ Jesus" (Philippians 4:7).

Patience

All of us have become impatient during a long drive. At some point, we've wanted just to be there already! We are so focused on our destination that we fail to appreciate the journey itself. God is able not only to help us to our destination but also to provide ample opportunities for personal growth and understanding along the way. He's able to give us patience because, after all, he's the author of patience! He has loved us and has been rooting for us since the creation of the world. Peter said a day is like a thousand years to God (2 Peter 3:8). At times, a single difficult day on our healing path can seem that long! God knows and understands.

Abby spent a solid year working through challenging and painful childhood memories. She told me it was the hardest year of her life, but one she wouldn't trade for anything. Remembering far more than she ever thought she could about the abuse in her past, Abby nevertheless didn't shrink from the task. She didn't try to make it less than what it was. Nor did she try to hurry the experience. Rather, she patiently allowed the work to proceed at its own pace, know-ing that healing lay at the end. She knew she'd learn a great deal about herself and her past. But the reason it was so precious to her was because she'd learned about God and his love for her. That under-standing was worth the wait, for it has transformed her life.

Be patient with the journey. Keep your destination in mind, but remember that God has wonders for you to see and experience along the way. To fully grasp what he wants you to learn, sometimes he says to you, "Be still, and know that I am God!" (Psalm 46:10). In other words, be still and be patient.

Kindness

Love and compassion seem like bright, bold words. At times, kindness can seem like a pastel word as in, *I was just being kind*. Kindness can seem like an after-thought to love and compassion. Yet here the word is in the midst of a list of vibrant spiritual blessings. Love is often exhibited through acts of kindness, and kindness from God is often linked with love in Scripture. Paul said we are saved through Christ because of God's goodness and "loving-kindness" (Titus 3:4). No, kindness is not an incidental word; it is a word ripe with power.

Consider the effects of simple acts of kindness in your own life and in the lives of others. Usually they appear as unexpected, out-of-the-ordinary gifts. Someone responding to a harsh word with a kind remark. Someone taking time to help a total stranger because he or she needed it at that moment. Someone noticing and responding to a forgotten or overlooked person. These have been called "random acts of kindness," but I venture to say they are not really random. Rather, these are the intentional acts of those empowered by the Spirit to administer the balm of kindness.

One more powerful thing about kindness: It not only warms the heart of the one who receives it, but it also warms the heart of the one who bestows it. Double blessings are surely the work of God.

Generosity

Being generous can appear to involve quite a bit of risk for someone who has been hurt, for when you are hurt, your reaction can be to roll yourself up in a protective ball and stay very closed. On the other hand, if you have a history of hurting others, your offers of generosity may be misinterpreted, and others may hold you at a distance. Either way, generosity can seem unnatural.

Don't let that deter you! Sometimes, when we're hurt, we know we must still give to others, but we do so sparingly and begrudgingly as if giving would increase our pain. Sometimes, when we've hurt others, we try to compensate for our behavior through excessive giving. Even though this is giving, it is not generous giving. Generosity means understanding the need and providing an ample portion. It places you in a reciprocal relationship with the one you're giving to, for generosity is responsive, not reactive.

✝ ✝ ✝

Faithfulness

In the midst of life, we can lose track of our resolve. That is why the attribute of faithfulness could be considered the engine for all the rest. Faithfulness— to God, to his Word, to his principles, and to your healing path—will keep you going when the going gets tough. Without it, forgetfulness can overtake us. John Eldredge talks about the danger of forgetfulness in his book, *The Journey of Desire*. He says of forgetfulness, "It cuts us off from our Life so slowly, we barely notice, until one day the blooms of our faith are suddenly gone" (200).

Because it is extremely easy to forget, we must be full of faith, filling up our reservoirs of faith through prayer, immersing ourselves in God's Word, connecting with the Holy Spirit, and pursuing a relationship with God in Christ. Not only will these things keep us on the right path, but they also will empower us on our journey.

Now, I understand that some may cite the severe circumstances of their lives as a reason why it is painfully difficult for them to hang on to their faith.

The sheer weight of their problems causes them to jettison faithfulness when the burden of life becomes too great. "Something's got to give," they say by way of explanation. If this is how you've responded in the past to the idea of being faithful, I can direct you only to the Cross. Use the faithfulness of Jesus as your model, for Jesus was faithful even unto death. In the Book of Revelation, we are told that if we can do likewise, we will be given "the crown of life" (Revelation 2:10). Faithfulness is not easy, but the rewards transcend this life to the next.

† † †

Gentleness

Why, of all the various noble attributes that could be included in the fruit of the Spirit, would God include gentleness? It seems, like kindness, to have a pale affect. Perhaps that is because we often look at things through the veil of this life. In our world, the gentle are often the misused. The gentle are those who are run over. The world's standard does not regard gentleness as something powerful. Yet, if we think about it, one of the most powerful emotions and one of the most powerful images is of a mother's love for her child. This love, though powerful, exudes gentleness. The touch of her hand upon her child's face. The gentle way she curves her arms to protect. The softness of the touch in no way diminishes the strength of her love.

We are confused about the power of gentleness. According to Proverbs 25:15, "a gentle tongue can break a bone" (NIV). Indeed, Jesus called himself "gentle" (Matthew 11:29). Gentleness involves an understanding of the other person or thing. It recognizes the inherent fragility of others and takes that into account. In the midst of pain, our immediate response can be vigorous and reactive. Yet, even then, God is able to help us respond in a thoughtful, gentle way. He knows that responding any other way can add fuel to the fire. In Proverbs 15:1, we are told, "A soft answer turns away wrath, but a harsh word stirs up anger." We have had enough anger in our lives; it's time for gentleness to turn away wrath.

Lord, I need your strength to be

gentle to others and to myself.

Help me understand gentleness

the way you do and not be con-

fused by the world's definition.

✝   ✝   ✝

Self-Control

It is an interesting paradox that God provides us with *self*-control. We assume that we are in charge of controlling ourselves. But we've been abysmal at it in the past! So much damage done in the world is because of our inability to control our own selves. We truly are the word picture in Proverbs 25:28: "Like a city breached, without walls, is one who lacks self-control." This is the essence of our fallen state: We are a breached city. God, however, is able to build up those walls and provide us with self-control through the Holy Spirit.

How do we achieve self-control? By looking completely outside ourselves for guidance. When confronted with an overwhelming situation, it is not enough to hope that our own fortitude or strength will uphold us and provide us with the answers we need to face the challenge. Rather, we must look to God for the way out of our situation. Further, we must actually do what he tells us. His commands are commands, not suggestions. When we give ourselves over to God's control, we will achieve control of self.

✝   ✝   ✝

A Transformed Mind

Full of the fruit of the Spirit, we are able to reclaim joy and contentment. With these comes the ability to respond to life in a positive, affirming way. We are able to participate again in the blessings of laughter and lightness of heart. Pain and suffering are so wearisome that we can forget what it is to smile and laugh. God does not want us to forget to laugh. Even Job, the sufferer of the Old Testament, said, "He will yet fill your mouth with laughter, and your lips with shouts of joy" (Job 8:21).

In this life, we will have pain and sorrow, but we should also have times of laughter and joy. Solomon in his great book on wisdom explains that our lives should not consist of sorrow to the exclusion of joy. Rather, he tells us that there is "a time to weep, and a time to laugh; a time to mourn, and a time to dance" (Ecclesiastes 3:4). In the midst of suffering, how can we find a reason to laugh? The psalmist answered that question by reminding us, "The Lord has done great things for us" (Psalm 126:3). God is our source of joy and laughter, as well as ultimate contentment.

A Transformed Body

In his book *Head First: The Biology of Hope*, Norman Cousins says, "Scientific evidence is accumulating to support the biblical axiom that 'a merry heart doeth good like a medicine'" (127). Laughter is not only good for the mind and spirit, but it is also good for the body. This thought brings us to the other casualty of the negative emotions—anger, fear, guilt, blame, and shame. The stress of these negative emotions robs us of vitality and physical well-being. The weight of these negative emotions can cause a downward spiral of health concerns that complicates our journey on the healing path.

Tony was over-the-hill and overweight. His doctor told him he needed to do something about it fast, or he was in for long-term health problems. Instead of motivating Tony, this news merely depressed him. The more depressed he became, the more he gave up. He didn't feel good about himself, and he just didn't feel good. When his doctor suggested he get some counseling, he thought it would be for nutrition. Tony assumed the problem was what he ate: He didn't realize the real problem was what was *eating him.* All his life, Tony had lived under the weight of unrealistic expectations, first from his parents, then from his peers, and then from his spouse. He'd been told so many times how worthless he was, how stupid he was, how he'd never amount to anything that Tony had come to believe it wholeheartedly. Because he never could envision anything to look forward to, he chose to live entirely in the moment. He was fat because food didn't disappoint him.

Amazing things are possible when a person is able to view themselves as God does. As Tony dealt with his perceptions, his optimism began to surface. He took to heart God's assurances of love and value. Tony began to take the tentative steps toward loving himself. He began to come out from under the cloud of his depression. His mood lifted, and he found he had the strength to engage in life again. Tony discovered the truth of Isaiah's words: "Those who wait for the Lord shall renew their strength, they shall mount up with wings like eagles, they shall run and not be weary, they shall walk and not faint" (Isaiah 40:31).

Many people do not recognize the tie between how you feel emotionally and how you feel physically. They are interwoven. When you are weighed down by negative emotions, it can be very difficult to find the motivation to take care of yourself physically.

God gave you your mind and your soul, certainly, but he also gave you your physical body. David, speaking of God, said, "For it was you who formed my inward parts; you knit me together in my mother's womb. . . . My frame was not hidden from you, when I was being made in secret, intricately woven in the depths of the earth" (Psalm 139:13, 15). This body has been called just a shell for the soul, as if it has no value on its own. While it is true that this body is temporary, God gave it to you to use on earth. He has physical activities for you to do that involve more than your mind!

Your body is a gift from God and one he intended for you to use for his glory. Paul was quite specific on this point: "Or do you not know that your body is a temple of the Holy Spirit within you, which you have from God, and that you are not your own?" (1 Corinthians 6:19). Everything about us belongs to God, including our bodies. He wants us to take care of the things he has given us, so they will be a blessing to us and so they can be used to bless others. Paul went on to say, "For you were bought with a price; therefore glorify God in your body" (1 Corinthians 6:20).

Too often, we cope with suffering in our lives through a denial or a numbing activity. We turn to alcohol, drugs, food, or sex to temporarily mask the pain. These activities become addictions and impede our progress on the healing path. That is why the apostle Paul admonished us in his second letter to the Corinthian church to "cleanse ourselves from every defilement of body and of spirit, making holiness perfect in the fear of God" (2 Corinthians 7:1). In order to fully heal, we must put our addictions behind us. I have seen many people find courage and strength in God, which has allowed them to overcome even years of chronic addictions.

For some of you who have suffered abuse, the idea that your body is a temple, able to be transformed by God, can be hard to accept. You may have come to hate your body and, therefore, mistreat it. Again I say our bodies do not belong to us; they belong to God. If, at this point, you cannot find it in yourself to take care of your body for yourself, can you take care of your body for Christ? Repeat the words of Paul in Galatians 2:20 about yourself: "And it is no longer I who live, but it is Christ who lives in me. And the life I now live in the flesh I live by faith in the Son of God, who loved me and gave himself for me."

No matter what has happened to you, no matter what you've done, God does not expect you to hate your body. Listen to what Paul said: "For no one ever hates his own body, but he nourishes and tenderly cares for it, just as Christ does for the church" (Ephesians 5:29).

As you continue on your journey to healing, please do not view your body as an adversary. Your body is an ally. When you nourish and strengthen it, you'll feel better physically. When you feel better physically, your mind and emotions will follow.

Father, you made my body. I confess I have not treated it as well as I should. Help me love and care for my body as you direct. I want it to be ready to give you glory.

God made us spiritual, emotional, and physical beings. As we trust him, he can transform each aspect. And all three are incorporated into our journey toward healing. As we experience the fruit of the Spirit in our lives, our minds are renewed, and we find the strength to respond to this world in a positive, uplifting way. When we acknowledge that God designed our bodies and knows best how to care for them, we will turn aside from the bondage of harmful addictions and free ourselves from their burdens. As we see God transforming our minds and our bodies through our obedience to him, our spirits are strengthened. Our trust in him grows, and we're ready to move beyond our pain toward healing.

One more joyous thought to consider: This work of transformation continues in this life and into the next. We are being renewed here in this life, and we will be transformed into his glory in the next. So, take heart and believe in your transformation, not because of anything you can do but because of everything God will do!

Chapter Six

Spiritual Intimacy

I Will Let Go and Let God Become My Best Friend

Few things in life are as traumatic or tragic as separation and loss. A parent abandons the home. A spouse starts a different life. Friends move. Children grow up and leave. A dream is shattered. Innocence is lost. Love dies. A loved one dies. Things change. Abandonment, grief, and loss are universal human experiences. Change itself defines living in this world. Those changes are not always eagerly anticipated or graciously accepted. They can be hurtful, devastating, and damaging. Healing from these losses is especially difficult.

Those people who are overwhelmed by loss can become sidetracked on their journey toward healing. For some, healing appears to diminish the depth of their loss. "Getting on with life" means leaving behind someone or something dearly loved. To them, healing becomes a negative, even a betrayal. They're so caught up in the past that it's a struggle to move beyond. Like a dog who will not leave the corpse of its master, people would rather stay with the loss.

For others dealing with the pain of loss or separation, healing is sidetracked when they succumb to hollow promises of false comfort. Leaving the true path to healing, they head down a side road, attracted by a sign that offers comfort, relief, and even oblivion. Some immediately follow this side road to false comfort while others take it as a way to endure the pain of living in the past.

† † †

Hollow Promises

While this world is full of loss, it also provides an ample supply of void-fillers. A loss is suffered, a void opens, and a plethora of fillers appear to plug the gap. What the world offers, however, can actually widen the rift, causing even more pain. Void-fillers come with a variety of names, but they share a common theme of addiction. There are the familiar: alcohol, drugs, sex, gambling, and eating disorders. There are also the subtle: when you're overly preoccupied with work, family, entertainment, money, or power. These things, as well as other things you can name for yourself, are void-fillers. They attempt to convince you that the void doesn't exist but ultimately fail because it does exist. With these counterfeit fillers, the gap may appear closed on the outside, but it grows deeper and wider on the inside.

Mary couldn't wait to get home. Work had been unbelievably stressful. She needed to unwind and forget about the accounting error she'd made and the yearly review coming up. As she drove home, however, her worries continued to hover at the back of her mind, pressing in. A part of her longed for the day when she wouldn't have to work and deal with other people's problems: She had enough of her own. But the reality of her situation was all too apparent. Single again, Mary had to work. Nobody else was looking out for her. Her husband was long gone and couldn't care less. Her kids were busy with their own lives and needs. So she was looking at years of work, struggling to do her best, constantly feeling stressed, and barely able to cope.

That's why she couldn't wait to get home. Her cat, at least, was happy to see her. He didn't want much—nothing she couldn't provide with a bowl and a can opener. Home meant relaxation. Home meant heading to the kitchen and fixing something to eat while she watched television. At one time in her life, Mary had zealously worried about her weight. Not anymore. It hadn't saved her marriage, and frankly she didn't have the energy. Food was comforting. Food was relaxing. She ate until she felt satisfied, not full; simple hunger no longer entered the picture. Sure, the pounds kept building, but she didn't care. The cat certainly didn't. Besides, who else was there?

Mary saw no reason to stop. Food felt good, and there were so few things that did anymore.

Hollow void-fillers are dead ends on the path to healing. They are a seductive sideshow, promising all the benefits of the main event. In truth, however, they are a stagnant eddy, sending you round and round in a tight little circle, with the appearance of motion but going nowhere. Their comfort is fleeting, deceptive, and confining.

When the pain of separation and loss hits, it can become a situation of "any port in a storm." When the winds blow and sleet pours down, our immediate thought is to find cover. We often seek a flimsy shelter we think will be temporary, but it ends up holding us long-term. Addictions are like this. After all, they are often chosen in the midst of a raging storm in our lives when their danger is weighed against the severity of the situation. We feel we need them, given the circumstances. The comforts are heightened, and the dangers minimized. Once we're within their grasp, they do not easily let go. Ask anyone who has struggled to overcome an addiction. Ask yourself; for all of us have behaviors and habits we use to numb the pain in our lives and distract us from dealing with the source of that pain. Some addictions might even be considered acceptable, like eating away our pain, or viewing away our pain, or reading away our pain, or sleeping away our pain. Whatever the addiction, we use it as a way to avoid the truth.

✝   ✝   ✝

Jesus, please give me courage to

embrace the truth. Allow me to

trust you with my pain instead of

finding ways to avoid it. Comfort

me in my pain, and give me your

hope to move beyond it.

✝   ✝   ✝

Letting Go of Loss

In *God Will Make a Way*, there is a strikingly simple statement: "Grief is accepting the reality of what is" (Cloud and Townsend, 210). Grief is often postponed in order to avoid the reality of loss. Because "what is" is lousy, we choose to avoid it. But in order to heal, loss must be grieved. Sorrow must be acknowledged and *accepted*.

The opposite of acceptance is denial. Reality and denial are at odds with each other. In order to heal, you must find a way around denial. One of the more persistent barriers to healing is the false idea that moving beyond a tragic loss in your life diminishes that loss. In other words, the only way to be true to the loss is to keep the wound fresh.

Donna came to me in a state of deep depression. Her beloved father had died several years earlier, and she'd never gotten over it. As she sat in my office, the only time her eyes showed any life was when she spoke about how wonderful her father was. He was the light of her life. He was the only one who ever treated her the way she wanted. Day after day, his loss haunted her. What would she do without him? Without him, who would think she was special?

It was this identity as "special" that bound Donna to her dead father. To her, grieving her loss and moving beyond meant giving up a valued part of who she was. When she buried her father, she felt that special part had died with him. Donna kept the wound of her father's death fresh because her true loss was in acknowledging she didn't feel special within her existing relationships. What Donna failed to recognize was the healing power of a relationship with God. To God, no one is more special than Donna, or you, or me.

† † †

Spiritual Intimacy

In order to really heal, we must recognize any dead ends we're in and rejoin the true path. Along this path, we walk in relationship with God. In a world of broken connections, God's promise of friendship binds us to him. In a world of unsteady relationships, God's steadfast love keeps us on firm ground. In a world of good-byes, God's presence is a continual "I'm here."

What I love about God is how he accepts and shapes us even when our relationships with others are broken. Addictions tell us that we must hide our true shape and that we must do whatever it takes to fill up the voids so they don't show. God doesn't try to deny the voids that happen when death, separation, and loss occur. Rather, he acknowledges the reality of our new shape and works within us to make that new shape whole. There is no need for an external patch, as if somehow you are defective after you've suffered. God doesn't try to pretend that the loss has not taken place. Instead of the void being patched over, you are made whole within the context of your new shape.

How are you changed and made whole again? He accomplishes this restoration through spiritual intimacy. This inside-out change is a benefit of the intimacy created through our relationship with God. He does this in a variety of ways, including the indwelling of the Holy Spirit.

God says when we are saved, we are given the Holy Spirit as a gift (Acts 2:38). He is called our Counselor (John 14:16) and the one who gives us comfort (Acts 9:31). God says the Holy Spirit will help us remember his words (John 14:16). The Holy Spirit is our constant companion, not separated from us, not forging out ahead, but choosing instead to take the journey with us at our pace, helping, guiding, and teaching us along the way. Before he left to return to the Father, Jesus reassured his disciples of the coming of the Holy Spirit (Luke 24:49). They were not disappointed, and neither are we. Jesus is faithful to his promise.

And with the Holy Spirit comes hope. Listen to two passages from Paul's letter to the Romans: "And hope does not disappoint us, because God's love has been poured into our hearts through the Holy Spirit that has been given to us" (Romans 5:5); and "May the God of hope fill you with all joy and peace in believing, so that you may abound in hope by the power of the Holy Spirit" (Romans 15:13). His Spirit is powerful and infuses our lives with hope.

We are also promised spiritual intimacy with Jesus, who is presented to us in Scripture as our husband-to-be (Matthew 9:15; John 3:29; Revelation 19:7; 21:9). In a beautiful passage in Ephesians, we are told how much Christ loves us as his bride: "Husbands, love your wives, just as Christ loved the church and gave himself up for her, in order to make her holy by cleansing her with the washing of water by the word, so as to present the church to himself in splendour, without a spot or wrinkle or anything of the kind—yes, so that she may be holy and without blemish" (Ephesians 5:25–27). Marriage is the essence of intimacy, and Jesus firmly established his desire for spiritual intimacy with us by presenting himself within the concept of marriage. Further, this isn't merely a convenient concept, for he has proven his love through his sacrificial death. He was willing to die for his beloved, and you are his beloved.

God's desire is to walk and talk with you intimately as he did with others we have read about in the Bible. Abraham, for example, is called God's friend in 2 Chronicles 20:7 and James 2:23. David is called a man after God's heart (Acts 13:22). It is important to note that even in the midst of Job's suffering, he acknowledged this special relationship with God: "Oh, for the days when I was in my prime, when God's intimate friendship blessed my house" (Job 29:4 NIV). Do you understand that God desires his intimate friendship with you to bless your house as well? The name may be different, but God's love and desire are the same. He loves you no less than Abraham, David, and Job.

Separation may be the way of the world, even when intimacy is present. Families split apart. Marriages end in divorce or death. Yet separation is not what God has in mind for our intimacy with him. This is why he chooses spiritual intimacy with us. Our bodies will perish, but our souls remain. Physical intimacy is God's temporal gift, which lasts for a season. Spiritual intimacy is God's eternal gift, which lasts forever.

As you struggle with the loss of separation, healing comes from knowing that God will never leave you. He has given you numerous promises that you will never be separated from him. They run the gamut from the Old Testament (Deuteronomy 31:6; Joshua 1:5; Psalm 73:23) to Jesus' promise at the end of Matthew: "And remember, I am with you always, to the end of the age" (Matthew 28:20). Our connection to God is kept strong through his power, not ours. It is his promise to us for this age and for the age to come.

Father, I have been hurt by loss
and separation in my life. I want to
come closer to you. Comfort me,
and give me the courage to
approach you without fear.

† † †

We have already spoken about the unique relationship God grants us as his children, having been
adopted into his household. This is truly the intimacy of close connection and familial ties. How
much more do you need to believe that God desires
spiritual intimacy with you? Instead, we focus on our
sins and fail to appreciate the relationship God
intended to have with us all along. It is a relationship
in which God walks and talks with us! I encourage
you to go back to Genesis 1 and 2 and read of the
closeness God and Adam enjoyed before Adam

disobeyed God. While sin entered to destroy that closeness, Christ died to restore it. This is an amazing concept, one many find difficult to accept.

✝ ✝ ✝

Fear of Spiritual Closeness

Jillian spent her childhood going to church. She knew about God but didn't really know God. As a teenager, she rebelled against her religious upbringing and wound up pregnant. The shame of her condition was more than she could bear, and after weeks of quiet panic, she obtained an abortion. The pregnancy was over, but her pain and fear continued to grow. She learned to live with it, eventually marrying and having children. At the birth of her first child, the guilt hit harder than ever. What was she to do? She'd gone back to church in order to give her kids the stability she had as a child. As she sang songs to them about how much Jesus loved them, the fear grew deep in her heart that he no longer loved her. After all, he knew what she'd done.

At some point, a person arrives at the truth: What he or she has been using to numb the pain no longer works. Further, it is causing its own pain. Many, at this point, will turn or return to God. But for some of you, this may not be simple or easy. Something is blocking your view of God, and it is difficult to find your way to him. I have found two prevalent obstacles facing a person who seeks to come closer to God. The first is the false idea that you have to be good before you can come to God, which we talked about in the first two chapters. The second is the false idea that God acts as your accuser. Nothing could be further from the truth.

With God as our ultimate healer, it is imperative that we draw ever closer to him. This "God as Accuser" label keeps many people chained to shame and fear, unable to accept spiritual intimacy with God. Where does this false idea come from? For many people, it comes from a warped image of God from within the religious institutions of their childhood. God was presented primarily as the righteous judge, all-knowing and ready to condemn the sinner.

For others, it comes from the personality of their earthly father or authority figure, who used a recitation of their faults to keep them shamed and controlled. However it comes, its origin lies in the deceiver, also called "the father of lies" (John 8:44).

A courtroom analogy is found in Romans 8:31–39. In this passage, God is called everything but accuser. We are told that God is for us, not against us (verse 31). We are told that God is a giver of good things to us, including Jesus (verse 32). In verse 33, we are told that God does not condemn us, rather he justifies us. Further, we are reminded that Christ, who took our sins, does not condemn us; he intercedes for us (verse 34). We are told all of this to assure us that we have a steadfast love in Christ. Ease your fears with the extraordinary words of verses 38 and 39, and say them personally in the first person: "For I am convinced that neither death, nor life, nor angels, nor rulers, nor things present, nor things to come, nor powers, nor height, nor depth, nor anything else in all creation, will be able to separate us from the love of God in Christ Jesus our Lord" (Romans 8:38–39). This promise is truly for you!

Walking and Talking Today

Spiritual intimacy with God is a healing balm that blesses our lives. We recognize our need for it. We acknowledge the ways we have been derailed from achieving it. So how do we intentionally reach out and grasp hold of it? Well, how do you develop intimacy with another person? Through spending time and sharing thoughts and a common purpose. It is no different with God. Another way to look at this is to see how you have gained spiritual intimacy through prayer (spending time with God), through his Word (sharing his thoughts as recorded in Scripture), and through obedience (accepting God's purposes as your own).

A wonderful aspect of this spiritual intimacy is that you can begin your relationship with God immediately, and it will be counted as valid. Then, as you mature and grow, your relationship with him will mature and grow in tandem. This is a lifelong, constant relationship. You can pour your heart and soul into it and not be disappointed or deceived. He will not forsake you. He cannot die. He has promised never to leave you. With God you are special and safe. Don't be afraid! The writer of Hebrews reminds us that we can enter into God's presence with "confidence" and "full assurance" (Hebrews 10:19, 22).

✝   ✝   ✝

Prayer

God wants to spend time with you. Granted, he is omniscient and omnipresent, so he knows everything and is everywhere, but spending time with you is a different concept. It has more to do with your focus than his characteristics. Another way to put it would be that he wants you to be God-focused during the course of your day. Prayer can be considered an ongoing dialogue with God. It is not just a recitation of requests or a series of complaints, though often that constitutes the bulk of our conversation with God.

Think of prayer as taking a long drive with a family member or friend. You don't spend every single moment talking; yet you remain aware of each other. You comment on things you see outside the car. You make plans about where you're going to stop and what you're going to do. You talk about what you're interested in or spend the time asking for insight about a difficult situation. You relish the journey together because your camaraderie is an important aspect of your enjoyment of the journey. This is especially true of our relationship with God.

If you find yourself at a loss to know how or what to pray, there are a couple of things you can try. Some people will form a mental picture of Jesus walking beside them as they go through their day. This allows them to comment and engage in a conversation as they would with a good friend. And considering Jesus as a friend is completely biblical, as we've seen. You might also obtain a journal. Many people have found great value in journaling their prayers as a way to remember and appreciate God's answers. They have been able to go back and note the date and time they wrote a prayer, and they have been astonished later on to see how God had responded before the prayer had even left their lips!

Still others have found it helpful to obtain a prayer journal written by someone else. Using these written prayers as models, they are able to develop a comfort level with their own prayers. For them, structured prayers provided a foundation as they grew more at ease with spontaneous prayer.

Some of you may seek a daily prayer time with God but are unsure how to begin or what to say. One of the most useful prayer aids I've learned is the ACTS method, which merely stands for Adoration, Confession, Thanksgiving, and Supplication. In other words, you begin your prayer by praising God for who he is; this is Adoration. Adoration sets the tone for your prayer as you recognize just who it is you are speaking to. Then, you acknowledge who you are; this is Confession. Confession is not meant to cause you shame but rather to allow you an opportunity to express regret, remorse, and repentance. With this attitude of contrition, God is able to mold your heart and fortify you for the future. Next, you count your blessings; this is Thanksgiving. It is important to remember as many positive things as you can! We certainly are bombarded enough by the negatives in the world. Taking a few moments to concentrate on all God has done for you is a refreshing, uplifting experience. You end by asking God for what you need, which is Supplication. This method has a way of clarifying not only what you pray for but also how you accept God's answer!

However you start, start. Keep focusing on God during your day. Talk to him as you would a friend. He knows everything about you (remember Psalm 139:1–6) and loves you with an unfathomable, demonstrated love!

✝ ✝ ✝

Integrating God's Word

Have you ever known a couple who have been married for many years? When they are together, they will often finish each other's sentences. So sure are they of what the other is thinking, they know what will be said after just a few words. This kind of deep connection and unity of thought is what God desires with us. I have known older Christians, who are so immersed in God's Word that they often will speak in a sort of scriptural language. In other words, as they seek to make themselves understood, they cannot help but use God's words. Their words stem from his. Scripture is the origin of their thoughts.

How can you be sure that what you are thinking is really what God is thinking? You have no further to look than the book of his thoughts he gave you, the Bible. He does not hide his thoughts from you. Taking great care, God made sure that you would have direct access to what he wants to tell you. He wrote it down, and you can read it in your own language. There are a myriad of Bible translations, taking into account all different styles, from the traditional King James Version, with which many people grew up, to the contemporary language version, *The Message*, by Eugene Peterson. You might find it valuable to read several different translations of the same verse or chapter, appreciating the nuances brought out in each. The Bible is a single book whose study can encompass a lifetime!

Charlie came to the Bible later in life than most. He grew up in the construction industry and spent more of his time poring over architectural plans and structural drawings than he did in the Bible. He left Bible study to his wife, Alice. When she died, Charlie found himself at loose ends. Because he was retired, all of his time had been taken up caring for Alice. After the funeral, he found himself with lots of time and no real idea what to do with it.

Going through a box of Alice's things, Charlie found one of her Bibles. She had several, but this one was well used. He remembered seeing her with it over the last ten years of her life. He'd picked it up as a connection to her, but over the course of the next year it had become his connection to God. He'd relied on Alice to do his talking to God; now he started talking to God for himself. While he still missed Alice deeply, he was excited about the new relationship in his life—his relationship with God.

† † †

Common Purpose

Intimacy is enhanced by experiencing a common purpose. People at odds with each other are rarely able to achieve true intimacy on a deep emotional

level. So how do you find a common purpose? It is
difficult enough with couples who truly love each
other. We are so different from God, how can we
achieve a common purpose? The answer is through
Christ. Listen to Paul, "If then there is any encouragement in Christ, any consolation from love, any
sharing in the Spirit, any compassion and sympathy,
make my joy complete: be of the same mind, having
the same love, being in full accord and of one mind"
(Philippians 2:1–2). Having the mind of Christ
allows us to bridge the gap between our own wants
and desires and the will of God.

Oh, we may want a common purpose with God,
but often we ask God to agree to our purposes. Rick
Warren says in the very beginning of his exceptional
book, *The Purpose Driven Life*, "It's not about you"
(17). Finding a common purpose with God is all
about God. You must trust him to know and understand the purposes that are perfectly suited for you.
This requires obedience, an invaluable component
of spiritual intimacy with God, for we know that
disobedience, or sin, separates us from God. Obedience keeps us in a love relationship with him. Jesus
put it quite simply: "If you love me, you will keep my
commandments" (John 14:15).

Does this mean that God no longer loves us when we are disobedient? Of course it doesn't! What it does mean is that a continual, willful pattern of disobedience and disrespect is as harmful to your relationship with God as it would be to another person. In *Fresh Encounter*, Henry Blackaby and Claude King deal with this concept of love and obedience. They write, "If you return to your first love, a love relationship with God, you will resolve the disobedience problems in your life" (78). Work on your loving relationship with God, and obedience will follow as a natural consequence.

We are not reaching for a perfect relationship with God; we're reaching for a relationship with a perfect God. Don't worry about trying to attain perfection; God's already got that covered. Just work on getting to know and love him more each and every day. This spiritual intimacy will allow his Spirit to reach down into your deepest pain and bring healing to your life.

Chapter Seven

Connections

I Will Let Go and Let God Direct My Relationships

What happens when you get your hand too close to a flame? Instantly, you draw your hand back. It's immediate. It's reactive. You get as far away from the source of the pain as you can. This reaction to physical pain is natural. And it also can be our reaction to emotional pain. When emotionally wounded, we tend to draw back into ourselves. We become suspicious of other people. We even become suspicious of our own motives and decisions. And so, we withdraw from people.

When a physical illness or disease strikes, our attention is immediately drawn inward as well.

Because we think we have to deal with the pain and the job of healing, we become so taxed, both physically and emotionally, that we feel incapable of interacting with others out of sheer exhaustion. Our lives often become so focused on our infirmity that healthy people have difficulty understanding. We're hurting. We're tired. We withdraw from people.

The net result is the same: isolation. Left alone in our pain, we are cut off from the healing touch that comes from our relationships.

Kathy agonized over her decision to seek a divorce from Mark. She tried counseling and was even able to convince Mark to go for a few sessions before that ended in abject failure. She knew the marriage was over but couldn't accept it. Back and forth she went, veering from despondency to hope, and back again. When she finally made the decision to end her marriage and start divorce proceedings, she thought things would get better. She thought she would get better, but she didn't.

Kathy was unprepared for the emotional roller coaster that came with dissolving a 17-year relationship. What to do about the kids? What to do with the house? What to do with all the things they'd gotten over the years? What to do with their investments? What to do with the dog? It was a nightmare. At some point, Kathy just went numb. She could no longer cry. She didn't even care anymore.

Coping became a strategy of apathetic acceptance. If it meant another call to the attorney, she made it. If it meant another legal document to sign, she signed it. If it meant getting her kids ready to spend the weekend with their dad, she bundled up their things and waved good-bye from the doorway. Kathy was locked in survival mode. No more tears. No more anguish. She told herself it was the only way to get through—the only way to survive.

Yet Kathy wasn't surviving inside; she was dying. No tears meant no laughter either. No more anguish meant no more joy. People became a burden. Most of her friends were married and couldn't understand what she was going through. Besides, they were busy with their own lives, and she had enough to do just to get through the day. Her home became her sanctuary. She stopped going to church. She just did her job and then came straight home. Slowly, her world shrank in on itself until it was only Kathy and her kids.

In the first book of the Bible, God said, "It is not good that the man should be alone"(Genesis 2:18). He was speaking in the context of the marriage relationship, but our need for connection is there, outside of marriage as well. We need extended family and good friends. Our connection to other people builds a closely knit community, and within the context of community, we are able to provide for the needs of others and receive help for our own needs.

In *Relationships*, we're reminded, "short of torture, society's worst punishment is solitary confinement" (Drs. Les and Leslie Parrott, 74). Why is it, then, that just when we need people the most, we tend to withdraw into ourselves? I believe there are several reasons, which either individually or in combination reinforce our belief that it's better for us to be alone with our pain: We think others won't understand what we're going through; we're distrustful of others because of what we've suffered; we're unwilling to forgive those who have added to our pain; we're so depleted that we think we have nothing to give to another person; because of what's happened to us, we don't believe we deserve to be loved again.

In each of the beliefs above, there is an element of truth. Yet it is only partial truth. Let's look at each of these beliefs, expanding our understanding so we can see them from a broader perspective. Ultimately, the truth is that we need others. If we are not able to embrace that truth, we sentence ourselves to the torment of solitary confinement. Invariably, we hurt ourselves even more.

† † †

The Community of Suffering

When calamity strikes us, it often does so when others around us are living calm lives. Like a tornado that touches down only on a single house in a subdivision, we are struck while everyone else is left standing. We feel marked, singled out, different. Our personal chaos takes place while others continue to live their everyday lives. The first question we ask is "Why me?"

When breast cancer hit at 32, Randi was caught completely off guard. She was young. This wasn't supposed to happen. When her hair began to fall out from the chemotherapy treatments, she felt strange no matter what she did to hide it. No wig, no hat, no scarf looked right. Angry that nothing seemed to work, she started making excuses for staying at home. If she couldn't conceal her baldness with a hat outdoors, she'd hide it by staying indoors. And it wasn't just external things like the hat. It seemed that when she did want to talk about the cancer, the person she was speaking to avoided the subject like the plague. If she didn't want to talk about it, sure enough, someone would call her up to find out how she was doing. At those times, the sympathy from healthy people was more than she could bear.

Living with deep pain can be an all-encompassing experience. The pain keeps drawing our focus back to itself. Inwardly focused, it's easy to believe that other people don't understand what we're going through. Our pain becomes a badge—a "C" for cancer, a "D" for divorce, an "L" for the loss of a loved one. The pain becomes our identity. So, as we look around at others who wear no such badge, we assume we have nothing in common. We feel alone.

As we've talked about, however, suffering is universal. Since many of us choose to suffer in private, we are often completely unaware of the individual paths to healing others have taken. We assume, since others appear normal, that nothing challenging or hurtful has happened to them. If we investigated further, we'd be amazed at the wealth of experience, help, and compassion that's available through others.

The solution is confession. James tells us that we are to "confess [our] sins to one another, and pray for one another, so that [we] may be healed" (James 5:16). Pain is not necessarily sin, though much of our pain comes because of sin. Yet confession is cleansing. We need to be open and honest with each other about the pain in our lives. We need to be willing to ask. When asked, we need to be willing to share. We need to be willing to pray for one another. This is the connection that brings healing.

Learning to Trust Again

Once we've been burned, we have a new appreciation for fire. While it is possible to avoid an open flame, it's not possible to avoid other people. And the sad truth is that others have burned many of us. It's the abandoned child who grows up to be aloof and distant. It's the left-behind spouse who determines never to let anyone get that close again. It's the used parent who builds a wall to keep from being taken advantage of again. Keeping people at arm's length, we operate under the principle that if an inch of separation is good, a foot is better; and if a foot is better, a yard is best. Bit by bit, we expand our protection zones, pushing out others. We think that if others can't come in, pain can't come in either. The terrible irony is that pain is already there. We brought it in with us, and we're excluding the very people who could comfort us in our pain.

So much of learning to trust again goes back to forgiveness. Again, without forgiveness, bitterness takes root. In *Holding On to Hope*, Nancy Guthrie puts it this way: "If you and I want to be free of the bitterness that estranges us from others and eats away at our own struggle to find joy again, we are going to have to forgive and pray for the friends who have let us down" (75–76). People both delight and disappoint. Flame both warms and burns. Avoiding the flame protects us from being burned, but we'll never be warm again. Forgiveness allows us to extend our hand toward the flame and enjoy the warmth again.

✝   ✝   ✝

Jesus, I've been burned, and it hurts. I want to be warmed again through relationships with other people, but I'm afraid. Help me forgive and trust again.

✝   ✝   ✝

When Nothing Is Really Something

When life overwhelms us, our reaction is to isolate ourselves. Just look at Elijah's reaction in 1 Kings 19. After defeating the prophets of Baal, Elijah flees for his life into the wilderness because of Jezebel's threat against him. Afraid and despondent, he pleads with God to end his life. After engaging in a valiant struggle against evil, Elijah doesn't celebrate, he hibernates (1 Kings 19:1–4). And we do the same thing.

Living through a crisis, either emotional or physical, can seem like engaging in a battle. Every day takes tremendous effort not only to survive but also to remain victorious. Each day is full of small skirmishes, each one draining our energy, resolve, optimism, and hope. While victory may be assured, the cost of that victory can be personally expensive. When the price is paid, we may truly believe we have nothing left to give to anyone else.

Our lives begin to feel like that children's game with sticks. You know, the one where you build up a maze of individual sticks, and each player in turn removes one. The object is to avoid being the one who takes out the stick holding up all the rest. You lose if you cause the house of sticks to fall down. Disappointment, abuse, neglect, disability, disease, loss—all of these remove sticks from our carefully constructed lives. When we are left in such a precarious state, interacting with others is like removing sticks. We're simply not willing to take the risk.

Ruth felt just like that. She had nothing left to give. To Ruth, being around other people meant giving to them. That's how she was raised and had lived her entire life. She'd given to her husband until he died. She'd given to her kids until they moved away. When she'd come down with depression, she kept it from her daughter and son, choosing instead to deal with it alone. When friends asked how she was, she said, "Fine." When people offered to bring her a meal or clean her house, Ruth's reaction was immediately negative. Her job was to give to others, not accept charity. The deeper her depression, the less Ruth had to give and the more she withdrew from her relationships.

Are we to be givers in our relationships? Yes! Will there be times in our relationships with others when they will need to give to us? Absolutely! The best and healthiest relationships are reciprocal, both give and take, as the occasion arises. None of us is immune to the challenges of life, and, when they arise, we need to draw upon the strength of others to persevere.

One of the beautiful ways God redeems difficulty is to make our experiences valuable to others. Listen to 2 Corinthians 1:4 in which we learn an important lesson about God, "who consoles us in all our affliction, so that we may be able to console those who are in any affliction with the consolation with which we ourselves are consoled by God." This passage shows a God who comforts, people who comfort, and people who will need to be comforted. It is unrealistic to think that we will always be the comforters and never the comforted. When we allow others to comfort us, we accept God's comfort through them! This is a blessing—to us and to them.

Ruth pushed away people who would have been blessed by ministering to her. Don't be afraid to ask for help. Don't be so prideful that you're ashamed of your need. Don't allow fatigue or exhaustion to derail your relationships. Allow others to build you up. Allow others to fill your needs. Allow others to remain in relationships with you. There will come a time when you will have the blessing of comforting others again because of what you've gained through this experience.

✝ ✝ ✝

Rejoining the Land of the Loved

One of the damaging aftereffects of a traumatic loss can be the devastation to self-esteem. We wonder, *After what has happened, can I ever be loved?* Too many times, we answer our own question in the negative. This is especially true in cases where abuse, abandonment, divorce, or death cause an existing relationship to end or substantially change. If we do not believe an uplifting, loving relationship exists in our future, it is difficult to find the motivation and momentum to heal. We feel cut off from the land of the loving.

Even those who are assured and know that God will continue to love them may still feel unsure that physical love or companionship is part of their future. But that's underestimating the power of love, which comes from God, who himself is identified as love in 1 John 4:8. God's love is powerful enough to understand the source of your pain. It is powerful enough to value you even with your pain. And it is powerful enough to help you see beyond your pain.

✝   ✝   ✝

Lord, grant me a vision of the
future that includes healing love.

✝   ✝   ✝

Don't Settle for Crumbs

After Pamela's abortion, she felt stained. Moreover, she felt incredibly stupid to have believed the promises of the man she loved. The promises had quickly evaporated, as had her belief that he had actually loved her and was going to marry her. She didn't want a child if she didn't have him. The decision was an easy one to make.

It wasn't so easy to live with, though. The abortion went against her religious upbringing. Deep inside, Pamela felt she'd blown it with God. He couldn't love her after what she'd done. She didn't deserve to be loved after this. But Pamela did so desperately want to be loved—to feel needed and wanted. Inside, though, she was unsure she was worthy of love. Feeling stained, she didn't think anyone would want her. Instead, she began to settle for feeling needed. And it wasn't hard to find needy men.

When our relationships are damaged, we can internalize the damage and feel compromised. When a relationship ends, the fear that it will never be replaced can take hold. In desperation, we sometimes settle for substitute relationships that are less than they should be. I have sat in my office and listened to people tell me that the lifeless or abusive relationship they have is all they deserve or should expect out of life. Feeling less, they settle for less.

God does not see you as less. He sees you as incredibly valuable. He does not grade on a curve, devaluing you as a person against the sins or saint-hood of others. Each person is his precious child. He does not want you to settle for less; he wants you to listen to him. His desire is to provide you with direction and guidance in all areas of your life, including your relationships.

An appropriate time to examine your existing relationships is while you're healing. You may find, as you have been walking in pain, that you have accepted any companion, any distraction. As you heal and realize that you are worth a life of love and affirmation, it's time to look around at those you have invited along on your journey. Do your rela-tionships help strengthen you and build you up? Or are they a drain on your life? Are your companions helping you move along, or are you expending all your energy carrying them? This, too, is a distrac-tion. It is so true that we often take on the burdens of others to avoid the reality of our own.

While it is good to be in relationships, not all relationships are equal. To heal, you may need to leave some of them behind. We are called to be wise in our relationships and choose those that are bene-ficial. Listen to Solomon in the Book of Proverbs: "The righteous gives good advice to friends, but the way of the wicked leads astray" (Proverbs 12:26) and "Whoever walks with the wise becomes wise, but the companion of fools suffers harm" (Proverbs 13:20). Choosing your relationships wisely is important! Remember that when God saw that it was not good for the man to be alone, he chose Adam's companion. He is willing to do the same for you if you will ask him for wisdom and give him permission to direct your relationships.

It can be difficult to accept that a relationship needs to be ended or altered in order for you to advance toward your desired goal of healing. If you are in a relationship that continues to cause you significant pain and injury, how can you reasonably expect yourself to heal? "Taking a stand against hurtful things that people do and against the things that are opposed to the life that God wants you to create is one of the most positive spiritual things that you can do" (*God Will Make a Way*, Cloud and Townsend, 153). If you find you don't have the strength and fortitude yourself to make these changes, know that God is behind you 100 percent. This is your life and your healing at stake. God's desire is for you to heal, and he understands that not all relationships, however well intentioned, work out.

Often, a draining relationship can be fixed. It can be changed to reflect a more reciprocal balance in which you are being filled as well as filling the other person. Like Ruth, you may need to examine how you have been approaching the relationship. If you have historically been the giver, it can come as a shock to the other person when that dynamic is changed. It can also be a pleasant shock, for that person may have been waiting to give back to you. This is often true for familial relationships. I've known of aging parents who, though uncomfortable at first with the role reversal, have been blessed by the care of their adult children. And their children are blessed to be able to give back some of the love and devotion they experienced from their parents.

† † †

Refilling Your Bucket

Sometimes unhealthy relationships need to be severed or severely restricted. While this can be perceived as another loss, it is also an opportunity. It is an opportunity to seek out a healthy, beneficial relationship to take its place. Don't be in a hurry. Allow the relationship to reveal its true nature over time. Be open about the pain in your past and your desire for healing. New friendships are a wonderful time to start fresh, not only with a new person but also with yourself. Each new friendship allows you to rewrite the definition of what it is to be your friend.

Recognize also that there are many types of relationships. There are acquaintances, friendships, romantic connections, and lovers. Depending upon where you are in your healing journey, some may not be wise or suitable. This doesn't mean you can't take advantage of the others.

But in all your relationships, God must be the guide. Ask yourself, "Is this a person God wants me to be in relationship with? Do the goals of this relationship match God's goals for me? If God was my earthly parent, is this someone I would take home for him to meet?" Our heavenly relationship must govern our earthly ones. They do not and cannot exist apart from each other. God cares about us, so it matters to him with whom we are spending time. It matters to him how we are treated and how we treat others. It's put this way in 2 Corinthians 6:14: "Do not be mismatched with unbelievers. For what partnership is there between righteousness and lawlessness? Or what fellowship is there between light and darkness?"

In your new relationships, choose people who practice doing right. Choose people who follow the light. If you're not sure, watch their deeds. Who they are will become evident. If you're still not sure, ask the Lord for wisdom and guidance. Ask him to reveal the person's heart to you. Ask God to reveal your own heart.

When we let go and let God guide our relationships, we demonstrate our love for and trust in him. Within the folds of a God-directed relationship, we are able to mend our broken hearts, exchange companionship for loneliness, and participate in the double blessing of helping others to heal and being healed ourselves. God sends us precious companions on our journey to healing. We were not meant to be alone. God can send each of us to encourage, rebuke, motivate, help, and love another person. Find this type of friend for yourself. Be this type of friend to others.

Chapter Eight

Vision

I Will Let Go and Let God Give Me a Future with Hope

In the midst of pain and suffering, the word "hope" is a cruel jab. When you feel crushed by the misery of the present, the word "future" bodes nothing but more of the same chill wind.

How did you feel when you read those words? Pressed down upon? Dispirited? Without hope? Did a part of you rebel against them? Did a part of you respond, "Surely that can't be true!"? Did a part of you stubbornly hold out for hope, even in the face of those despairing words? My prayer is that each of you could answer this last question with a "yes," even if it was only a very small "yes." That "yes" represents a flicker of hope. When the circumstances of life press in on you, wrap your heart and your faith around that flicker of hope. Take heart in knowing that others, when faced with trials and suffering, were able to do the same. Indeed, some of the greatest triumphs of hope in the midst of suffering come from the Bible.

In Eugene Peterson's introduction to the Book of Lamentations in *The Message Remix*, he writes, "It comes as no surprise then to find that our Holy Scriptures, immersed as they are in the human condition, provide extensive witness to suffering" (1477). In fact, the Old Testament books of Jeremiah and Lamentations are filled with some of the bleakest descriptions of suffering and despair ever penned. Yet in the midst of these solemn depictions of utter devastation come two exquisite passages of hope, like diamonds in the midst of ashes. After reciting an extensive litany of his own suffering, Jeremiah said something perfectly understandable and then something astonishing. First, he spoke of his suffering: "My soul continually thinks of it and is bowed down within me" (Lamentations 3:20). All of us have felt this way: bowed down because of our suffering. Yet Jeremiah doesn't stop there. He continued, "But this I call to mind, and therefore I have hope: The steadfast love of the Lord never ceases, his mercies never come to an end; they are new every morning; great is your faithfulness. 'The Lord is my portion,' says my soul, 'therefore I will hope in him'" (verses 21–24). Even in the midst of long-term, catastrophic suffering and devastation, Jeremiah still spoke of God's love and mercy, with hope!

Jeremiah was able to give the people of Israel this ray of hope: "For surely I know the plans I have for you, says the Lord, plans for your welfare and not for harm, to give you a future with hope" (Jeremiah 29:11).

How could these words of promise and hope come in the midst of such suffering? Because God is more powerful than the source of our pain. He is able to take the suffering we all experience and turn our pain into personal and spiritual gain. Understanding this allowed James to make this seemingly absurd statement: "My brothers and sisters, whenever you face trials of any kind, consider it nothing but joy" (James 1:2). Joy in the midst of trials of *any* kind? "How can that possibly be?" you ask. "Because you know that the testing of your faith produces endurance; and let endurance have its full effect, so that you may be mature and complete, lacking in nothing," James responds (verses 3–4).

In commenting on these verses, Bruce Wilkinson agrees that this is a difficult concept, and we will understand it "only when we understand that the reason we are to count it all joy is not because of the experience, but because of the *result* of the experience" (*The Dream Giver*, 120). God is not the author of suffering; he is not the author of the experience. He is, however, the author of the result, if we allow him to be. And when God is able to redeem the results of our suffering, we experience healing.

✝   ✝   ✝

Gary had carefully constructed a seemingly successful life. With his strength of will and driving personality, Gary built all the proper components—a thriving business, a beautiful wife, gifted children, and good health. These components lasted well through his 30s and into his 40s, and then they began to unravel.

Over the years, his wife started to grow distant. She said it was all the time he spent away, taking care of his business interests. Gary's kids became teenagers, and the control he'd exerted upon them as children evaporated in the heat of their own desires. The business continued to do well, but the stress of daily operations wore Gary down. His health suffered.

When his son was found to have a drug addiction, Gary was furious and terrified. This wasn't the way life was supposed to be. This wasn't what he'd worked so hard for all these years. Instead of coming together, Gary and his wife fought over who was ultimately responsible. Attorney fees, rehab expenses, and treatment costs ate away at their savings. Stress mounted; Gary's health declined further.

The same month he laid off a third of his sales force, Gary suffered a heart attack. He found himself saying, "What now, Lord? What else can happen?" Gary couldn't understand why all this was happening to him, why God was allowing it to occur. After all, hadn't he done everything he was supposed to do in taking care of his family? Life was falling apart around him—his son was messed up, his daughter had left home, his wife barely spoke to him anymore, his business was struggling, and he couldn't even count on his own strength to fix things.

One night, it became too much. When his wife came into their bedroom to tell him something, Gary began to weep, feeling like a failure, like nothing was ever going to be right again. He'd given his best years to get this far, and he didn't have the strength to put it all back together. All he could see was his life falling apart.

That night was Gary's turning point. His wife, who had felt so distant, so removed from him, found her way back as they grieved together over the losses they'd suffered. For the first time, Gary empathized with the consequences his son was dealing with. Instead of being angry with his daughter for "abandoning ship," he just wanted to see her again. The business transformed back into just that—a business, not a reflection of his own ego. Letting it all fall around him, Gary began to sort through the debris of his life to look for the important pieces—God, faith, and family.

✝   ✝   ✝

In the book *How People Grow*, Drs. Henry Cloud and John Townsend talk about the coping mechanisms we use to handle the stresses in our lives. These coping mechanisms are often forged in childhood, and we continue operating under them well into adulthood. Sometimes, though, we need to let go of these coping mechanisms in order to grow. "Trials and suffering push those mechanisms past the breaking point so we find out where we need to grow. Then true spiritual growth begins at deeper levels, and we are healed" (213). Through the trials Gary suffered, he came to understand areas of his life where he needed to grow, areas he'd never even considered. While he experienced painful trials,

God was able to redeem those experiences for good by producing a spiritually beneficial result. When this happened, healing happened.

Gary's trials were personal. Some of you will relate to them, and others won't. While the negative experiences of suffering and trials vary from person to person, the positive results through God are universal. He is able to take your experience and redeem it for your good. Knowing this, you will come closer to considering your trials and accepting them with "joy." If you're having trouble envisioning a day when you can truly count your troubles as treasures, don't be discouraged. This is a difficult concept, learned over a life of trials and of trusting God.

Lord, I want to learn to trust you

and turn my trials over to you so I

can experience healing.

Multifocusing

Most of you have heard the term "multitasking." It describes the ability to do several things at once. There are those who would say we simply can't get along without it! If multitasking is beneficial, consider the value of "multifocusing." By this, I mean the ability to see one thing from several different perspectives, specifically the perspectives of past, present, and future.

When suffering or trials occur in our lives, they tend to telescope our view into a preoccupation with the present. Physical and emotional pain can be so overwhelming that they demand our complete and immediate attention. The here and now supercedes all other views. While this is natural for a short period of time, it can be damaging if we maintain this singular focus over the long-term. Why? Because focusing solely on the present robs us of the lessons of the past and the hope for the future.

When we're hurting, pain seems the only clear lens. When we're hurting, we look at our past, which can seem a bleak landscape. Our current suffering appears to be a dreary constant. Pain fills our past and overwhelms our present. Is it any wonder we ignore the future, believing the pain will continue indefinitely? We may appear to be multifocusing, but we're concentrating on the negative and failing to take the positive into account. Only through multifocusing on God are we able to pay attention to the present and still gain benefit from both the past and the future.

Let's look again at the passage from Lamentations, this time from the point of view of multifocusing: "My soul continually thinks of it and is bowed down within me. But this I call to mind, and therefore I have hope: The steadfast love of the Lord never ceases, his mercies never come to an end; they are new every morning; great is your faithfulness. 'The Lord is my portion,' says my soul, 'therefore I will hope in him.'" Jeremiah spoke of the present and his soul as being "bowed down within me." He was aware of his present condition and also of his past sufferings. Nevertheless, Jeremiah put them into context. He spoke of being able to "call to mind" or remember a past when "the steadfast love of the Lord never ceases." The past to Jeremiah was not merely a litany of injustices and trials, it was filled with evidence of

God's love and mercy. With a foundation of God's past deliverance, Jeremiah saw a positive future, one in which God's mercies would be "new every morning." Firmly rooted in the past, present, and future, Jeremiah had hope. In order to hope and in order to heal, God must be our continuum.

If Jeremiah could find hope in you,

Father, so can I. Help me see the

love and mercy you give me every

day of my life.

✝   ✝   ✝

A Future with Hope

When we remain broken, hurting, and in pain, it is difficult to move forward. While we might be moving forward in time, we remain stuck in the immediacy of our pain. Healing, however, propels us past the pain. Healing gives us the ability to claim our future. One of the wonderful truths is that healing, even in stages, is beneficial and brings blessings.

Margaret was rocked by the death of her mother, brother, and aunt, all within the same year. Mother first, then her brother five months later, and her aunt four months after that. The pain of their deaths built up such a barrier that Margaret found herself unable to move beyond that year. Time went on, life went on, but Margaret stayed behind emotionally. Finally, her family convinced her she needed help dealing with her losses. Her daughter told her, "Mom, all of us feel we lost you, too, last year." Margaret realized she had lost herself, buried under grief.

Through a series of stages, Margaret realized her view of the future had changed with these deaths. She was so focused on the pain that all she could see ahead were future losses. How would she feel when her husband died, when her father died, or, God forbid, if one of her children died before her? How would she ever survive such a future? One of her most significant steps to healing was when she acknowledged that, deep down, she hadn't lost her faith in God but she had lost her trust in a loving God. If he'd taken these people she'd loved so dearly today, how could she trust him tomorrow?

Margaret needed to regain sight of Jeremiah 29:11 in which we are promised that God plans not to harm us but to give us a future with hope. True, Margaret had been focusing on her present pain and on her past, but she needed to go back and look at the total picture of her past, at the losses and at how God had cared for her, guided her, and protected her through them. She needed to remember the promises he had given her. She needed to acknowledge her anger toward God and to reach out to him to restore their relationship. When she did, God redeemed her pain. Margaret now facilitates a recovery group at her church, where she helps others come to grips with the death of a loved one within the context of a loving God.

Margaret learned a valuable lesson, articulated this way by Rick Warren in *The Purpose Driven Life:* "Your greatest life messages and your most effective ministry will come out of your deepest hurts" (275). One of the stunning ways God can redeem your painful past and turn it into a future with hope is through connecting your pain to his plan. This gives a positive purpose to your negative pain. God, knowing that we would sin, was fully aware from the creation of the world that tears and pain would enter the world. Accepting this truth, he found a way beyond the pain by redeeming it in his service. Simply put, God takes our suffering and uses it to his glory and the benefit of other people. Listen to Paul, who said, "I consider that the sufferings of this present time are not worth comparing with the glory about to be revealed to us" (Romans 8:18). This is the Paul who knew physical, emotional, and spiritual suffering. His focus, however, was not on his suffering but on the glory to come—a future with hope.

When we persevere through suffering while trusting him, God is glorified. When we pass through our pain and emerge strengthened in spirit, we are better able to help and be more attuned to others who are suffering. With God's help, our sufferings produce a bountiful harvest. This is the promise given in Psalm 126:5–6: "May those who sow in tears reap with shouts of joy. Those who go out weeping, bearing the seed for sowing, shall come home with shouts of joy, carrying their sheaves."

Here Comes the Sun

Please know that it is God's desire for you to experience healing. Whether your trials are physical, emotional, or spiritual, you are not alone. God is with you. Charles Swindoll, in *Hope Again*, says something that really hits home: "No matter how dark the clouds, the sun will eventually pierce the darkness and dispel it; no matter how heavy the rain, the sun will ultimately prevail to hang a rainbow in the sky" (277).

Living in the Pacific Northwest, I have seen incredible rainbows. Double bows of vibrant, sky-arching color bursting forth at the merest hint of sun after a violent rain. I see them, and I smile, for I believe in their promise. I believe in their confirmation of a loving God who announces the sun after the rain with such celebration! Do you know that God wants you to experience the same celebration of healing in your life? The same touch of the sun after the rain? From the dreariness and darkness of your pain, God wants to send forth his rainbow of healing and bring you joy so you can be a witness to the world of his love and power.

For those wearied by the burden of suffering, listen to these promises:

Psalm 30:5: "Weeping may linger for the night, but joy comes with the morning." God in no way seeks to minimize your pain. He recognizes that in this world there will be weeping. It is his desire, however, to hedge that pain within a specific time frame and follow it with joy. Depending upon the source of your pain, your healing journey may be longer or shorter than another healing journey. But please know that God has joy for you at the end. Please, keep going. Please, keep moving toward healing! Your destination awaits; it is not in doubt if you only will keep moving forward.

Proverbs 23:18: "Surely there is a future, and your hope will not be cut off." In the midst of pain, it can feel as if your hope has been cut off. You're so sure you'll never feel anything like joy again. This is not true as this verse clearly states. There is not merely a future hope for you, there is *surely* a future hope for you! God has promised that he will not allow that hope to be cut off. And who is more powerful than God? Once promised to you, who can take your hope away from you? No one but yourself by failing to claim it.

Job 11:17–18: "Your life will be brighter than the noonday; its darkness will be like the morning. And you will have confidence, because there is hope; you will be protected and take your rest in safety." Because there is hope, your future is secure. Even Job, the example of ultimate suffering, could say these words. If he can, so can you.

† † †

Waiting in Hope

Mike lives in a body distorted by cerebral palsy. His mind is fine; he's intelligent and engaging and has a wonderful sense of humor. But his body twists and turns in upon itself with random jerks and contortions. When asked what he hopes for, Mike says, "A new body." He doesn't really *say* it because Mike is not able to speak. Instead, his clubbed hand with outstretched thumb must jab at a word pad. After Mike labors for a stretch of time, a disembodied, mechanical voice says, "A new body."

Lowell came down with cancer. It was Lowell's deepest wish, and that of his family and friends all across the country, that he be healed. He did everything in this world to secure it. Over and over he prayed for it. When the answer came, it wasn't what he expected. Near the end of his life, Lowell told a dear, lifelong friend that God would heal him, but he knew it would be only through death. Death, he said, was his deliverance and his healing.

How do you wait in hope when what you hope for is not possible in this world? For some of you with physical impairments, disabilities, or disease, complete physical healing will not come this side of heaven. For some of you, with deep emotional scars and psychic traumas, complete emotional healing will not come this side of heaven. In the midst of this truth, God must still be sufficient.

Mike longs for a new body, and he has been promised one, but he has longer to wait. Lowell wanted healing here; he has it in heaven. Even knowing their suffering, Mike and Lowell would join to tell you the words of Psalm 33:20–21: "Our soul waits for the Lord; he is our help and shield. Our heart is glad in him, because we trust in his holy name."

Mike, living daily in physical suffering, would say to us, "Rejoice in hope, be patient in suffering, persevere in prayer" (Romans 12:12).

Lowell, dying from cancer, could finally say, "For God alone my soul waits in silence; for my hope is from him" (Psalm 62:5).

In truth, with the pain and suffering of sin and death, this world is never going to be a place of ultimate healing. That realm is reserved for heaven, where it is said that God "...will wipe every tear from their eyes. Death will be no more; mourning and crying and pain will be no more, for the first things have passed away" (Revelation 21:4).

In the meantime, however, God has promised to be with us. He has given us his Son. He has given us his Spirit. He has provisions to comfort us through the love, lives, and examples of other people. God lives. Hope lives. "And hope does not disappoint us, because God's love has been poured into our hearts through the Holy Spirit that has been given to us" (Romans 5:5).

In some ways, I wish I could tell you that your current suffering is your last suffering. This simply isn't true. What I can tell you is that God is able to sustain you through your suffering and help you find your way to healing. It may not be the complete healing of heaven, but it will be sufficient for now in this world. And each time you successfully navigate your way through suffering to healing, it will be easier to find the path the next time. For there will be a next time, and a time after that. And each time, God will be with you. Look for him in the rainbow, in the comfort of others, in the example of Jesus, in the whisper of your prayers, in the certainty of his Word, in the presence of his Spirit, and in the touch of his love.

Thank you, heavenly Father, for your loving presence in my life. Please bring me healing here on earth. Thank you for the promised joy of heaven.

Epilogue

God's healing touches every kind of wound. Whether we suffer from a psychological disorder, physical affliction, or emotional trauma, God is always available to be our kind physician and understanding counselor. The following three stories provide clear evidence of his amazing compassion and healing power.

† † †

Amber

Amber smiled and leaned back against the picnic table, watching her two young children playing in the park. Overcast skies left a touch of warmth in the air. It was so peaceful that Amber couldn't help smiling. But the peace she felt wasn't merely because of the early spring afternoon or from hearing the happy sounds of children swooshing down slides and trampling over play equipment. It was peaceful outside, yes; but for the first time in a long time, it was also peaceful *inside*. Healed from her inner turmoil, Amber was finally at peace with herself.

It was funny, she thought, how quiet it was inside. She'd lived so long with the background noise of her troubled thoughts that she'd failed to realize how loud and disruptive they'd become. She was free now from those destructive mental conversations she used to have with herself. She used to live on constant rewind, playing back conversations and arguments, past and present, and it didn't matter whether it was with a parent, sibling, or coworker. Amber couldn't let anything go, not an actual or perceived slight or disagreement. She'd examine each situation with focused intensity, reliving the moment and reliving the anger. In her mental reenactment, however, Amber also made sure to come up with an appropriately devastating comment to verbally skewer the other person. She'd think about it, test it, and deliver it with perverse pleasure, relishing her secret revenge. Instead of satisfying her inner rage, these conversations kept that rage lit, glowing and ready to flare at any opportunity.

No one else knew about these inner dialogues; she never shared them. On the outside, Amber kept herself in check, thinking she was disguising how she really felt. To others, though, Amber always seemed tense, uneasy, and volatile, as though she was never really happy. When she realized how often she vented her anger on her children, Amber knew she needed to change.

The first thing Amber needed to do was acknowledge how angry she really was. She always considered that the source of her anger was mistreatment or misunderstanding on the part of other people. It came as a shock to her when she realized that the source of her anger wasn't any of those things—the source of Amber's anger was Amber.

At first, she was frightened and devastated because of the depths of her anger. Really looking at it—at herself—wasn't easy. She had to accept this as an aspect of her character—she was an angry person. But because of God's love, Amber came to see that she was an angry person who could change.

With the focus of her life on God and not on herself, change and healing took place. With God as her focus, Amber could wake up in the morning and be optimistic about the blessings God had in store for her. Since it was his purposes she was fulfilling, she could turn to him for guidance when difficulties or challenges arose. When getting her way was no longer the only acceptable result of every encounter, every encounter ceased to be a battle. She could relax and put down her shield of hypervigilance. Instead of the drumbeats of warfare, Amber could hear the laughter of her children, the tenderness of her husband, the assurances of her God, and the peace of her own heart.

Patrick

Patrick didn't have time to worry about his health. All of his energy was absorbed in his career and getting ahead. He ate what he wanted as a way of rewarding himself. After all, he worked hard. He should be able to eat what he liked even if it meant becoming extremely obese. Since the other areas of his life were about sacrifice, he wasn't about to sacrifice where food was concerned.

Unfortunately for Patrick, his doctor didn't agree with him. Looking at his obesity, his stress level, and his resistance to change, his doctor was blunt—if Patrick didn't make changes, he'd be dead of a heart attack within 20 years. After hearing those words, the only change Patrick considered was in doctors. He politely listened and then left the office, determined to live the way he always had.

Over the course of the next year, two major events took place that caused Patrick to be more receptive to his doctor's advice. First, Patrick suffered a back injury. He was loading groceries into his car and bent the wrong way. It felt like a knife had been inserted firmly between his shoulder blades. He was off of work and on muscle relaxants for a week. Second, Patrick's company was downsizing, merging with another company. Everyone's job was being looked at closely and evaluated. Patrick felt even more stress over his job performance. But as his desire to work even harder increased, his energy level just didn't seem to be there.

As his personal life became shakier, Patrick reached out for some stability by going to church, and he found himself actually looking forward to services. A men's breakfast group started up, and Patrick decided to join. They met early, which would not interfere with work, and the networking just might come in handy. At first, it was strange to talk to other men about spiritual things, but slowly he began to open up about his life and work. One morning, the discussion focused on how each man's relationship with his own father affected how he saw himself and God.

Without really knowing where his thoughts were leading, Patrick began to talk. He spoke about what it was like growing up with a demanding father and always feeling like it was impossible to be good enough. He admitted he'd always put God at arm's length, fearful of getting too close. The thought of having one more stress in his life—the need to per-form spiritually along with everything else—seemed like a headache Patrick wasn't willing to risk. The more he thought about it, the more he realized how stress was overtaking his life. He felt he was drown-ing in it and didn't know how much longer he could tread the surface.

Patrick also realized he hadn't really put much personal emphasis on his own role as a father; he basically let his wife make most of the decisions with their kids. His main drive in life had been his work, but now he realized he had more important reasons to get up in the morning. With the dust settling from the merger, Patrick determined to do his best at work. At the same time, he knew whether or not his job was eliminated was not solely dependent upon him. A paycheck just wasn't worth missing out on his kids' future.

Patrick also started listening to his wife and made an appointment to go back and talk to his doctor. He recognized he needed to rethink how he was living his life. Patrick's weight decreased, and he started to feel more energetic. The doctor recommended some back exercises, and Patrick actually began to do them. It became apparent that a great deal of his emotional stress was contributing to the physical stress in his back. Patrick kept up the exercises, watched how he was handling stress at work, and felt his back getting better and better. Most of all, though, he continued with his men's group. The spiritual guidance and strength it gave him fueled his desire and ability to heal and make changes. His wife and his children are happier than they've been in a long time.

† † †

Judy

During Judy's entire life, people seemed to look first at her physical appearance. Tall for her age and for a woman, Judy never did melt into the background. Because she was big and athletic throughout high school, Judy had many male friends. But she had no boyfriends. She was the one boys would talk to when they were having trouble with their girlfriends. It hurt, but what could she do? She just figured things would change as she got older.

During college, Judy took a job at a small video store. The store was open late into the evening, the hours were flexible, and there was plenty of "dead" time for doing homework. One night, as Judy was closing up the store for the night, she didn't realize she was locking in trouble. A male customer had hidden within the store, waiting until closing. Startled and frightened, Judy was raped. Her first sexual encounter was one of violence, force, and terror.

Judy healed physically from the assault rather quickly, and as soon as the bruises healed on the outside, Judy thought she had healed on the inside. She hadn't, though. Over the next ten years, the scarring of the rape continued to work deeper and deeper into Judy's psyche. True to form, the effects were noticed outwardly, for Judy put on more and more weight. She went from athletic to fat and from tall to large. If anything, she became even less "feminine" than before. She used her height and size and her absence of emotional response to isolate herself from others. Taking a technical job, Judy was able to keep contact with people to a minimum.

After the rape, Judy no longer viewed men as potential companions and certainly not as potential lovers. The only men she came into contact with were professional colleagues. As long as she did her job well, with her weight providing a protective barrier, that's precisely how things would stay. Judy was fine with this arrangement until well into her thirties.

But her weight became more of a problem as her emotional relationship shifted to food. Always focused, intense, and successful in the business world, as well as being a committed Christian, Judy couldn't understand why she couldn't pray herself to thinness. Nothing seemed to be working, and she kept getting bigger and bigger, more isolated, and more lonely.

Desperate, Judy found a female therapist—one who shared her Christian values—to work with. Knowing her relationship with food had over-stepped its God-given boundaries, she was ready to be healed. There were times when Judy almost quit, faced with the depths of her injury, an injury she'd been able to mask over with a variety of coping mechanisms, including food. Angry at God, she refused to speak to him for almost a year. But her counselor kept reminding her that God loved her and wanted her whole.

Starting from that belief and that conviction, Judy slowly moved toward healing by having the courage and self-confidence to disengage from her dangerous relationship with food and transfer her emotional needs to God. Her faith grew, and her body shrank.

Soon, people commented on her outward appearance. They were amazed at the weight she was losing. Judy opened up to them. Her appearance had been a shield around her in the past; now, it became an open door, inviting others in to hear the story of how God's love was changing her life.

† † †

You

You've just read Amber's, Patrick's, and Judy's stories. Now, what about you? Your story of spiritual healing is just waiting to be written! God loves you just as much as he loves Amber, Patrick, and Judy. His mercies are available to you in the same supply.

As we come to the end of this book, I want you to know that your story lies ahead. God is willing and able to do amazing things in your life! Please trust him, rely on him, and cling to him. God loves you, and he wants you to have joy in him, peace in yourself, and contentment with your life. All of these are possible! I have seen it over and over again in the lives of Ambers, Patricks, and Judys. Go out, trust God, and see it in your own life! May God bless you.

† † †

Loving God, I so want to be
healed. Please help me look to you
for the wisdom to know how to
change, for the strength to make
the change, and for the grace to
sustain the change. May my healed
life be a witness to your mercy and
love in my life! Amen.

† † †